The Divided World
of the Bolivian Andes

The Divided World of the Bolivian Andes
A Structural View of Domination and Resistance

Dwight R. Hahn
John Carroll University
University Heights, Ohio, USA

CRANE RUSSAK
A member of the Taylor & Francis Group
New York • Philadelphia • Washington • London

USA	Publishing Office:	Taylor & Francis New York, Inc. 79 Madison Ave., New York, NY 10016-7892
	Sales Office:	Taylor & Francis Inc. 1900 Frost Road, Bristol, PA 19007-1598
UK		Taylor & Francis Ltd. 4 John St., London WC1N 2ET

THE DIVIDED WORLD OF THE BOLIVIAN ANDES: A Structural View of Domination and Resistance

Copyright © 1992 Taylor & Francis New York, Inc. All rights reserved. Printed in the United States of America. Except as permitted under the United States Copyright Act of 1976, no part of this publication may be reproduced or distributed in any form or by any means, or stored in a database or retrieval system, without the prior written permission of the publisher.

1 2 3 4 5 6 7 8 9 0   BRBR   9 8 7 6 5 4 3 2 1

This book was set in Times Roman by Hemisphere Publishing. The editors were Heather Jefferson and Corinne Naden; the production supervisor was Peggy M. Rote; and the typesetter was Cynthia B. Mynhier. Cover design by Berg Design.
Printing and binding by Braun-Brumfield, Inc.

A CIP catalog record for this book is available from the British Library.

Library of Congress Cataloging-in-Publication Data

Hahn, Dwight R.
   The divided world of the Bolivian Andes : a structural view of domination and resistance / Dwight R. Hahn.
      p. cm.
   Includes bibliographical references and index.

    1. Peasantry—Bolivia—History. 2. Peasantry—Government policy—Bolivia—History. 3. Agriculture—Economic aspects—Bolivia—History. 4. Land reform—Bolivia. 5. Bolivia—Politics and government—1952-1982. 6. Bolivia—Politics and government—1982-I. title.
HD1531.B6H34   1991
305.5′633′0984—dc20   90-46742
                                                                                          CIP

ISBN 0-8448-1695-7

To Suzana and Nicholas

Contents

Preface		ix
Acknowledgments		xi
Chapter 1	**Introduction: Case Study and Organization**	1
	The Meaning of *Campesinado* in Bolivia	3
	Case Study and Application of Theory	4
	Chapter Organization	6
Chapter 2	**Modes of Production, Class Place, and Ideology**	9
	Mode of Production	9
	Articulation of Modes	11
	Ideology, Class Place, and Social Change	14
	Application to Bolivia	21
	Dominant, Preexisting, and New Ideologies	22
	Preconditions for the Intrusion of Capitalism and Immediate and External Processes of Production	24
	Conclusion	26
Chapter 3	**Original Characteristics of the Indigenous Social Formation and Its Articulation with Capitalism**	31
	Class Place	32
	The *Ayllu*	34
	Incan Social Formation	35
	Knowledge and Class	39
	Spanish Colonization	41

	Spanish Administration	42
	Resistance and Rebellion	45
	The Republic	47
	Effects on the Indigenous Communities (*Ayllus*)	49
	Hacienda as Point of Economic Articulation and Political Control	51
	Indigenous Rebellions	53
	Conclusion	53
Chapter 4	**Review of Postrevolutionary Bolivian Politics**	**59**
	Social Blocs and Political Developments	60
	Prerevolution Politics	63
	Revolution and Outcomes	68
	Postreform Peasant-State Politics	72
	Conclusion	81
Chapter 5	**Structural Results of Agrarian Reform**	**85**
	Articulation and Disarticulation	87
	Articulation: Seasonal Migration to Zones of Capitalist Production	90
	Disarticulation: Basis of Ideological Division of Modes of Production	94
	Conclusion	97
Chapter 6	**Mode of Production, Class, and Dominant Ideology of the *Campesinado***	**101**
	Problem of Ethnicity and Class	104
	Class Place of Direct Producer	109
	Indigenous Nonproducers	115
	Ideological Unification	117
	Special Condition of Ideology in Noncapitalist Mode of Production	118
	Tin Miners	119
	Bolivian State and State Policy	119
	Conclusion	122
Chapter 7	**Conclusions**	**127**
Bibliography		135
Index		141

Preface

Bolivian resident and scholar Javier Albó observed that centuries ago, in 1781, the city of La Paz, Bolivia, was blockaded by a ring of thousands of Aymara Indians. Nearly two centuries later, in December 1979, the *gente decente* of La Paz probably relived something of the panic of their forebears as the *indiada* once again blockaded the city in protest over economic measures implemented by the Bolivian government (1987). Once again, perhaps for just a moment in the temporary isolation brought by the blockade, the *blanco* population perceived themselves as strangers upon an alien land.

By incorporating political and ideological elements into a modes-of-production analysis, this work seeks to provide a structural understanding of the ongoing clash of two cultures in the Bolivian Andes. Although the arrival of the Spanish to the Andes in the 1530s resulted in the destruction of the Incan ruling class and its political apparatus, the basic building block of the Incan social formation—the *ayllu* (and its leadership and indigenous ideological practices)—remained intact, even as it was required by the Spanish to turn its ideological and political practices to benefit the ruling class on the Spanish side of the new social formation. The continued existence of indigenous social relations and a tenuously co-opted indigenous leadership helped assure that indigenous ideology was able to drive periodic rebellions against the domination of the Spanish and Bolivian ruling class of the Republic.

The most recent rebellion of the indigenous side was that which resulted in the 1953 agrarian reform. For two-thirds of the indigenous population immediately previous to the agrarian reform of 1953, the hacienda system acted as a mechanism for attaching its labor power to the creole side of the formation. The nature of this mechanism was such that neither noncapitalist relations of production nor ideological practices were eliminated. Following the dissolution of the hacienda system of economic and political control, the indigenous laborer was disattached from any process of labor relating to the capitalist mode of production as long as he or she physically stayed in the indigenous zone. For most, capitalist social relations remained alien. Left on its own, the *indígena* (indigenous population) became, for the most part, a class of small-holding agriculturalists tending to self-sufficiency, placing assured survival ahead of risk in the marketplace (i.e., a "peasantry"). Nonetheless, the Bolivian state, acting from economic imperatives after the decline of mining in the early 1980s, sought to displace the noncapitalist peasantry with commercial farming.

Demonstrating that the post-1953 era of *indígena* and Bolivian government cooperation had truly ended, a new indigenous leadership rejected the attempts at displacement. The *katarista* movement in general, and the leadership of the Confederación Sindical Unica de Trabajadores Campesinos de Bolivia (CSUTCB) in particular, led the indigenous opposition to the Bolivian government. At its 1986 national congress, calling upon the names of *indígena* "martyrs" for guidance along the road to "true national and social liberation," the CSUTCB made clear its intentions to struggle for the maintenance of political independence of the *indígena*. As the Bolivian government and other agencies attempted projects of rural "development," the *indígena* had its own conceptions of social transformation and it was apt to forcefully refuse the imposition of "development" that would result in its own demise as a separate social entity.

Dwight R. Hahn

Acknowledgments

I thank the many people in the United States and Bolivia who helped me put this work together. Upon my arrival in Cochabamba, Bolivia, I benefited greatly from the friendly assistance and frank discussions of Alberto Rivera and Jorge Dandler of CERES. My thanks as well to Susana Rance and the people at CEDOIN who allowed me the use of their extensive collection of newspaper clippings. There were also a number of people in Bolivia whose friendship and interest helped me to better know that country. In particular, I thank Cristina Arcos, Teresa Lynn Anello, Brian Johnson, Garth Pollack, and Eli and Bernardo Fritzsche.

I also thank Professors Mel Gurtov and Michael Kearney for their commentaries on the manuscript during its development as a dissertation. I am especially grateful to Professor Ronald Chilcote who helped me chart a path into a complex field of literature. I also greatly appreciate the skills, warmth, and friendship of Joan Littlejohn.

I also wish to acknowledge the financial support of the University of California at Riverside and the Organization of American States (OAS). A grant from the chancellor's Patent Fund bought me a ticket to Bolivia. A fellowship from the OAS provided generously for my living expenses in that country and paid for my return trip to California as well.

Chapter 1

Introduction: Case Study and Organization

When Bolivia makes U.S. media headlines, it is most often with stories of coca production and the ensuing politics of U.S. attempts at "elimination at the source." Rarely does the North American audience get a glimpse of the extraordinary culture of Bolivia. Once in a while, however, such an article does appear in the popular media. While putting the final touches on this manuscript, I happened across an AP wire service story in a local newspaper. The story concerned the Aymara Indians of Coroma, Bolivia, who were awaiting a U.S. court decision regarding the export of several of their sacred weavings to the United States. The Aymaras maintained that the weavings had been illegally removed from Bolivia and that the weavings belonged to them. The interest of the Aymaras was not historical, nor was it purely religious. The article quoted one of the Aymaras: "The textiles are the collective property of the community. . . . They are the spirit of the community. Because they were lost, people have died or lost their eyesight. There is drought and many animals have died." A Bolivian psychologist, quoted as an expert on the Indian community, added that the weavings were used to communicate with ancestors and that this communication was essential to the political and social well-being of the community: "The ancestors orient or direct the community in resolving political, social and individual problems" (*San Gabriel Valley Tribune,* June 15, 1990, p. E2).

This story of conflict between dealers in "antiquities" and Aymaras who lived that "antiquity" presents something of a microcosm of the Bolivian social formation. Representing some 35 percent of the total population of Bolivia,[1] the rural peasant farmers of the altiplano and Andean valleys are mostly ethnic Aymaras and Quechuas who live and breathe a reality far different from that of the capitalist world, which has been ideologically and economically structured by the descendants of Europeans. In 1950, 1,000,000 Bolivians spoke only Quechua, and 664,000 spoke only Aymara. As late as 1976, over one fifth of the population spoke no Spanish at all. In rural areas 17.1 percent of the men and 27.4 percent of the women spoke only Quechua; 8.2 percent of the men and 15.9 percent of the women spoke only Aymara (Albó, "Lengua y sociedad en Bolivia 1976," Instituto Nacional Estatistica 1980).

In Bolivian society there is a major division, but it is not just between the rich and the poor, the workers and the owners, or the peasant and the landowner. Bolivia's major division is between two worlds in which values, perceptions, and social organization are radically different. To understand this division and political outcomes, this book applies modes-of-production analysis to the Bolivian social formation.[2] For this study, a mode of production is considered to be composed of three interlocking aspects or features. These features—the political, the ideological, and the economic—should be seen as the pervasive themes that, together, combine in various effects, which in turn compose the reproducing thing called society. These aspects are not just mutually cohesive (or intra-articulative); they are also interarticulative; they are the focal areas that can and do link with other modes of production. This notion of interarticulation helps us, as social theorists, explain such situations as the encounter of capitalist with noncapitalist societies.

In the Bolivian case, the capitalist mode of production came to dominate an original or indigenous system of production in the sense that capitalism benefitted from the extraction of surplus value from the indigenous side, but political and ideological domination was uncertain, if not altogether lacking. The tenuous nature of this domination makes this case particularly interesting. Historically, the indigenous population of the Bolivian Andes periodically engaged in rebellion against the Spanish and their Bolivian descendants. Furthermore, the Bolivian land reform of 1953, far from helping the two systems meld or bring about the dissipation of the one into the other, made the political connection or articulation between them more problematic than in the immediate past, even as it became perhaps the single remaining link of the three points of articulation. Because of this, especially as the decline in the tin market in the mid-1980s compelled the Bolivian government to attempt further intrusion into the indigenous side, the indigenous mode of production became a potential candidate for a peasant-based revolution in opposition to the capitalist side.

Further, this theory of modal interarticulation helps us to explain the persistence of many peasant communities as they faced what was supposed to be the onslaught of "modernization." In fact, the major hypothesis of my initial research design when approaching the post-1953 Bolivian peasant question for a dissertation project was that capitalist farming was developing among the formerly noncapitalist farmers—or indigenous peasantry. I felt this was an appropriate hypothesis primarily because the legal conditions for noncapitalist production had been broken by decree in 1953. Nearly 40 years after the reform, one would think that if capitalism were developing in the *campo* (countryside) we would at least see the seedlings if not the harvest. However, while unearthing the details of the Bolivian experience during a one-year stay in that country, it became apparent that the *campesinado* itself was not opting for capitalism, and Bolivian capitalism did not appear to have the capacity of intruding directly into the indigenous zones.[3] The 1953 agrarian reform should not be seen, as I had originally considered it, as a step in the breakup of noncapitalist farming. Although it is certainly true that the reform placed Bolivian *campesinos* into relations of property and labor wholly different from the conditions in which most of them had lived, the effects of the new relationships were far from clear.

The 1953 reform clearly represented a victory for the *campesinado,* which had joined forces with miners and the Movimiento Nacionalista Revolucionario (MNR) in 1952 to overthrow the old oligarchy. The *campesinos,* for the most part, gained their stated goals—ownership of land and state-recognized (legal) control of their own labor. Beyond the economic implications, the fact of this political self-assertion led me to a consideration of the political history of the *campesinado* within the Bolivian social formation. This history is permeated by the effects of ideological factors that are at the heart of a division of the European/capitalist side and the indigenous/noncapitalist side of the social formation.

THE MEANING OF *CAMPESINADO* IN BOLIVIA

The very use of the word *campesinado* in Bolivia signals the existence of the two worlds that make up that country. As used in Bolivia, *campesino* does not easily translate to the word "peasant." The first difficulty is that the word is not used to distinguish between a person who works a small plot of land, tending to self-sufficiency, and a "farmer" who is commercial or market-oriented. As *campesino* is used in Bolivia, it would be more accurate to translate the term as meaning an inhabitant of the countryside (its literal translation to English from the word *campo* or countryside); whether that inhabitant be a peasant, a craftsperson, a rural merchant, or, perhaps most significantly, a farmer. Although the term *agricultor* is used and is applied to the capitalist farmer in Bolivia—especia.. ·/ to those of European heritage—the use of the term *campesino* has obscured the distinction in English between "peasant" and "farmer."

This slurring of the distinction between peasant and farmer in Bolivia is in part brought about by the fact that the term signifies not simply those that inhabit the countryside but all those who are *of* (in the sense of from) the countryside as well. This leads to the second aspect of the term as it is perhaps uniquely used in Bolivia where the word *campesino* came to replace the word *indio*. *Campesino* became an ethnic designation as much as, if not more than, a designation of occupation. This use became official speech after the 1952 revolution with the intention of dignifying the ethnic category of Indian. The word *indio* in Bolivia developed from its origins as a European misnomer of an ethnic category into a term of derision. When *campesino* replaced *indio,* it did not (as an English speaker might think) subtract from the ethnic significance that the original term carried. In some ways, the term *campesino*—viewed by the English speaker in its more literal translation as person of the countryside—is a more accurate rendition of the term *indio* without the latter's derogatory connotations. That is, both terms were used to signify those people who were of and remained a part of the "indigenous way of life"; those people who, in a sense, were indigenous to the land of which the Europeans and their descendants were alien.

The *campesino,* then, is something more than a reference to occupation, or even a lifestyle bound to an occupation. The word, as used in Bolivia, refers to an ethnic designation—Indian. Because the word *campesino* incorporates the word *indio,* the best meaning of either term in the Bolivian context is that—which many Bolivians began using in the 1980s—of *indígena,* or "indigenous person."

The reason for stressing this interpretation of *campesino* is that we, as social observers, should be alerted to the fact that the Bolivian *campesino* cannot be placed in any paradigm that considers him or her to be engaged in primitive agricultural practices and who is in need of some "modernizing" transformation. The Bolivian *campesinado* is living in the "modern" world. The point, however, is that it is their world and not the European world. Furthermore, the Bolivian Indian is more than simply ethnically different from the European. Probably because of their control of the land, the Indians of the altiplano and Andean valleys were able to maintain distinct economic, political, and ideological relations among themselves. The articulations and the disarticulations of those relations with the European side of the Bolivian social formation are the focus of this study.

CASE STUDY AND APPLICATION OF THEORY

The purpose of a case study is to apply a body of theory that may have been developed in the contemplation of various concrete situations. This does not mean, however, that theory should take the form of categorization and predetermine the character of the case studied. A single case study such as this one is not for the purpose of determining whether or not this case can fit into neat, ideal types or categories. The study of the particular should be done in an attempt to uncover and explain certain processes (selected for by the theory) within that particular situation. It should not be done to prove or disprove the merits of a particular category of, say, an associative and possibly causal relationship between category A and category B that, to prove true, must react the same in country (i.e., test tube) X as it did in countries Y and Z. That is, a case study should not be the purely deductive application of some preexisting typology; neither can or should it be strictly inductive. The method of analysis attempted in this study of Bolivia allows examination of social processes by applying tools (as opposed to categories) of analysis. This is not to say that these tools cannot be applied in cross-country studies, but the findings—the "categories"— are not necessarily generalizable. The overriding consideration here is that mode (and ensuing class) analysis requires a case study approach, or, at least, a case-by-case study approach.

The theoretical framework for pursuing an examination of Bolivian agrarian economic and political processes, as first tentatively applied and then developed, was a product of various ideas regarding articulation of noncapitalist modes of production with capitalist modes of production, class, and differentiation. Gradually, a cohesive explanation for the Bolivian situation emerged. The initial application of the theory itself determined on what general features of the Bolivian social formation my research would concentrate. This initial examination, in turn, helped refine the initial concepts I was using. This, in turn, reshaped the historical features upon which the analysis focused.

I contend that the apparent survival of peasant production is best formulated and explained with the concepts found in the "modes-of-production" and "articulation" theories. Modes-of-production theory enjoyed a resurgence of use in Third World studies because of its theoretical ability of taking an apparent noncapitalist (or, more specifically, a "peasant") mode of production seriously. Unlike modernization theory or traditional Marxian analysis, this body of theory (at least that which I develop and use here) allowed social observers to make analytically useful distinctions between capitalist and noncapitalist modes of production, which could then be used to account for the unexpected persistence of noncapitalist modes of production and help to explain the political and ideological predicaments of the social formations in which they persist.

The conceptual element of articulation in this body of theory directs the observer's attention to the interaction or "articulation" between the two (or more) modes of production, which in turn compose the given social formation. Through the use of this theoretical framework to describe and explain the dynamics and the conditions of existence of a noncapitalist mode of production in

Bolivia, this study reveals and focuses upon a basic structural contradiction within the Bolivian social formation.

CHAPTER ORGANIZATION

The chapter organization of this book is based upon divisions among historical periods, structural explanation of the postagrarian reform period, theory, and conclusions. Some of the more important theoretical concepts are explained in the relative isolation of Chapter 2. These concepts are then used and developed in an examination of the pre-1952 Incan and Bolivian social formation in Chapter 3, which begins its historical coverage with the pre-Columbian Incan period and contrasts this to the changes brought about by the "articulations" between the modes of production of the Spanish and indigenous groups. I also include the Republican period in this chapter.

Chapter 4 is a review of the political history of Bolivia from the period in which political conditions and alliances were established that precipitated the 1952 revolution. Of special importance, this chapter covers the development of the politics between the state and *campesinado* into the mid-1980s. The overview of the post-1952 political situation in Bolivia presented in Chapter 4 is then "structurally" examined in the next two chapters. Chapter 5 contains a detailed analysis of the structural changes and type of economic articulation brought about by the 1953 agrarian land reform. Chapter 6 applies the theoretical analysis of a structural account of ideology to the politics of the post-reform *campesinado*. Among other concerns, these chapters grapple with the matter of whether the *campesinado* qua indigenous ethnic group should be considered a homogeneous group capable of unified political action. That is, what is the "objective" class condition of the *campesinado* and what is the relation to its political position? This, in turn, leads to Chapter 7, which contains a few words on conclusions, a review of the study, and some thoughts on the politics of Bolivia.

NOTES

1. This figure is derived from the following data: of the total estimated Bolivian population for 1985, 42.2 percent were placed in the category of *pequeños agricultores* (small farmer—indicating peasant farmer) and the breakdown of population involved in agricultural activity across region was 60 percent in the altiplano, of whom 76.9 percent were "small farmers"; 20 percent in the valleys, of whom 79.4 percent were small

farmers; and 20 percent in the plains of eastern Bolivia, of whom 50 percent were small farmers (*Fundo Internacional de Desarrollo Agricola* (FIDA) 1985, p. 8 and World Bank 1984, p. vi).

2. Defined in Chapter 2, a social formation refers to the historical "reality," which is analyzed through the more abstract concept of modes of production.

3. By the term "indigenous zones," I refer to those areas of Bolivia where the peasantry (qua Indian) has remained on the land. Although the labor of this agricultural group of indigenous people (or *indígenas*) was directly expropriated by the Spanish of the colonial period and by the *hacendados* of the Republican period, the *indígena* remained in control of his or her land. In this way, the agrarian reform—as argued in Chapter 4—was a reassertion of that control over the land and of individual labor.

Chapter 2
Modes of Production, Class Place, and Ideology

This chapter introduces modes-of-production theory and discusses the processes that make up a mode of production. Borrowing from Nicos Poulantzas, I define a mode of production as a reference to an interrelated combination of economic, political, and ideological processes. I also make use of Poulantzas' explanation of "class place" in terms of the intersection of these processes.[1] The ideological and political elements of the articulation process in the social formation of Bolivia have combined to determine (or to structure) the class place of an "intermediary"[2] class location. In order to prepare the way for the analysis of this class place, this chapter goes into some detail to explain Poulantzas' use of political and ideological criteria to determine the category within monopoly capitalism of the "new petty bourgeoisie." In Chapters 3, 5, and 6, I make use of this analysis to explain the structural determination of the intermediary class place variously occupied by Incan nobility (functioning as bureaucrats and priests), *kurakas,* and peasant union (or *sindicato*) leaders. The special importance of this class place is that it resides upon something of a San Andreas fault. That is, the area of this intermediary class has been the area of rupture between the two modes in the events of ideologically driven political disarticulation (manifested historically in rebellions and "uncooperative" peasant organizations and leadership).

MODE OF PRODUCTION

The concept of mode of production used here refers to an articulated complex of three processes—ideological, political, and economic. A mode of production should be viewed as an abstraction or mental construct initially drawn from "historical reality." This "reality" is mentally reimposed by the social observer to explain processes that exist within history. Such a view construes the world as being a social product (of the interaction of minds with the external—including other minds) where reality is ideologically and politically "structured." However, such a structure can be stepped out of, examined from a new vantage point, and reinterpreted through "theoretical practice"[3] (and, perhaps, even consciously acted upon).

A simple, though apt, analogy might be seen in the manner in which the mathematician abstracts pure geometric forms from the external "reality," and through the use of those abstractions is able to further analyze and manipulate the "objective" world. The mathematician can never point to an object in the observed world and correctly say, "this object is a triangle." He or she can only say, "this object, examined via the concept of geometric form, is *triangular.*" That is, the sides meet at three points, the angles are of a certain sum, and so on. (This geometric form demonstrates the "processes" of what is called a "triangle.") In the same way, the social scientist can never correctly point to an observable process (in history) and say, "this is a mode of production that is capitalism." It would be more accurate to say, for example, "this given social formation, examined via the concept of mode of production, exhibits a process that we call capitalist. It also exhibits processes that we have called . . . ." The term "mode of production" (like the term "geometric form") refers to a mental construct and not to some directly observable "thing." Rather, the concept of a mode of production is the equivalent of the notion of geometric form; how a particular geometric form can be described depends upon the observations made via the application of the concept of geometric form. The final labeling of the form (e.g., triangle, hexagon, etc.) is irrelevant to the discovering of the geometric "processes" that determine the components of form.

An important implication for methodology here is that it makes little sense to speak of a "typology" of modes of productions. The term "mode of production" refers to an abstracted process and not to a label. It does not make sense to argue that there is a set number of kinds of modes of production (e.g., asiatic, feudalist, capitalist, socialist). Rather, a mode of production is a process that can be analyzed by discerning and examining various component relations and production processes, involving the overall reproduction of the given social formation. In my use of the concept of mode of production, these relations are political, ideological, and economic, which—at least in a capitalist mode of production—are joined or articulated within the immediate process of production. Whereas it is useful or convenient to label certain processes that have combined to form similar structural relations, say, capitalist and other feudalist, that convenience should not be confused with the object (or the objective) of the analysis. It is not my intention, for example, to determine what label to give to the mode of production associated with the Incan polity.[4] Modes-of-production analysis is not a project of determining into which preexisting category (label) a process should be placed. Modes-of-production analysis is in direct opposition to the logic of the analysis of "typology." The category cannot be used to define the process; at best, the process might define the label (where the label is used as a shorthand reference to the process).[5]

This analysis has pervasive implications. For example, the concept of class should be viewed as designating social relations that result from specific processes and that to understand class (or "class place") is to understand those processes. A further implication here involves comparative analysis more generally. As discussed in Chapter 1, the logical order of a cross-country (social formation) analysis would flow from the particular process to, if at all, the descriptive category. It would not make sense to begin from the cross-country, descriptive category and work to the particular (especially if that is taken to mean simply a small sample of the same category). For example, it does not make sense to argue that the labeling of phenomenon zzz in country X is invalid because it does not meet the "criteria" "established" for the category of zzz in countries A and B.

An implication of the dialectical roots of modes theory regards the flow of causality. Ultimately, within this view, everything is related to everything else. This should not be taken to an extreme that would leave us unable to make meaningful statements about particular relationships of association, reflection, and mutual causality. For example, Resnick and Wolff (1987) made a great deal out of opposing "essentialist" analyses of "reality" with their notion of "overdetermination," which they take from Althusser and Freud. The notion of "overdetermination," if taken to the extreme that Resnick and Wolff seem to want to take it, results in the analysis that everything is related to everything else. Although that may be true, it does not help us much to say that A is determined by Z just as A is determined by B because A is "overdetermined" by B through Z. We cannot make statements such as A affects B, but we can make such statements as A affects B as B affects A.

ARTICULATION OF MODES

My use of the concept of mode of production is derived from the explanation provided by Poulantzas, in which "the concept mode of production itself . . . embraces relations of production, political relations, and ideological relations." "Social formations" for Poulantzas were the "concrete result" of the "articulation of relations" with other modes. European capitalist societies at the start of the twentieth century, according to Poulantzas, were combinations of various modes and "forms": feudal, simple commodity production, competitive, and monopoly capitalist (1978, p. 22). Further, Poulantzas argued that social formations were usually dominated by a particular mode of production "which produces complex effects of dissolution and conservation on the other modes of production" (1978, p. 22). He allowed, however, that there is an exception: "The one exception is the case of societies in transition, which are, on the contrary, characterized by an equilibrium between the various modes and forms of production (1978, p. 22)." One methodological implication here, especially in examining a possible case of a "society in transition," is that the analysis of a social formation should concentrate on the sites or points of articulation in order to provide a structural understanding of the social formation. That is, the structural articulations (and disarticulations) are as important, if not more so, than the content—say, of an ideology—within a social formation for an understanding of the dynamics of a social formation.

This is to say that when dealing in modes-of-production analysis, we are concerned with structural connections. When applying the theory in an analysis of an encounter of one mode of production with another, we are concerned with the points and effects of that articulation on the reproduction process of the ensuing social formation. One can readily see how this theory developed as a response to world systems and dependency theory. The historical question of the non-European world's encounter with capitalism (or precapitalist merchant activity) and the underdevelopment of the Third World involves a linkage between these two worlds for the transfer of value from the Third World to the merchant and capitalist system of the expanding European economy. Dependency theory then concentrated on markets as the major point of articulation between the two worlds and, thus, the explanation for underdevelopment. This focus on the *inter*national aspect of development and underdevelopment, though, was unsatisfactory for an account of the effects on the class structure and politics within Third World countries.

One purpose in using modes-of-production theory is to make use of its capacity to direct analysis away from the market as the primary nodal point of articulation (which is where dependency theory would center its analysis) to the political and ideological aspects of this articulation. Poulantzas' analysis of modes of production is a major step in this direction. His inclusion of the political and ideological elements within the process of production (and thus part of the relations of production) provided the idea of how to construct a definition of class place that was created in the process of articulation (within the process of reproduction) of the capitalist and noncapitalist modes of production. This analysis then shifts us away from the economic perspective of dependency theory to more explicitly political questions.

Another purpose in using modes theory is to take advantage of its apparent usefulness in explaining the persistence of noncapitalist relations of production in Bolivia. The notion that the articulation of modes of production could result in the reinforcement of noncapitalist modes, for example, was examined by Pierre-Philipe Rey, who used and developed modes-of-production theory in African studies. In his summary of the "modes-of-production debate," Aiden Foster-Carter (1978) credited Rey as being the first to use the idea of articulation between or among different modes of production within the same social formation:

> Rey's original insight "is that capitalism can never immediately and totally eliminate the preceding modes of production, nor above all the relations of exploitation which characterize these modes of production. On the contrary, during an entire period it must reinforce these relations of exploitation, since it is only this development which permits its own provisioning of goods coming from these modes of production or with men driven from these modes of production and therefore compelled to sell their labor power to capitalism in order to survive" (Rey; cited in Foster-Carter 1978).

An important issue that emerges here is how, or even if, this articulation results in the implanting of capitalist relations of production (capitalism) into the noncapitalist mode of production. Relations of production constitute the "internal" of a mode of production, and, to speak metaphorically, the integrity of a mode of production remains intact as long as its own social relations of production remain intact. If relations of production become capitalist (characterized by wage labor, dispossession of the means of production, and economic coercion), then that mode of production probably should be characterized as capitalist. Historically, the encounter between capitalist and noncapitalist modes has not always meant the development of capitalist relations of production. Most observers, however, have considered that the capitalist mode involved in such a process of articulation with a noncapitalist mode of production is dominant—in the sense that one side gains through the economic exploitation of the other and that the noncapitalist side is eventually exhausted.[6]

An important question regarding the Bolivian situation is the matter of whether the indigenous side of the social formation is to be inevitably absorbed into the capitalist side. At least one Bolivian scholar, Silvia Rivera Cusicanqui, rejected modes-of-production theory because (among other reasons) of its apparent bias against the survival of noncapitalist modes of production (November 1985 interview). Rivera's view, and that of the "*katarista* movement" in Bolivia, was that the indigenous population of Bolivia (especially those of the Aymara group of the altiplano, though the claim was made for all indigenous groups) was an economic and cultural entity exploited by, but capable of survival and triumph over, the oppressive system of capitalism brought by the Europeans to South America (see, e.g., Rivera Cusicanqui 1984; Javier Hurtado 1986).

IDEOLOGY, CLASS PLACE, AND SOCIAL CHANGE

An especially important aspect of Poulantzas' work is his inclusion of ideological and political elements in the concept of the mode of production: "The concept mode of production itself . . . embraces relations of production, political relations and ideological relations" (1978, p. 22). This inclusion of the ideological and the political as "determining elements" of a mode of production is significant to the analysis of class place and "articulation" between or among two or more modes of production.

In a commonly accepted sense of "dominant ideology," it is viewed as a structure that is interrelated to the economic structures (class—social relations of production) and political structures (class and state—relations of political domination) of a given social formation. It is structural in the sense that it is an "objective" phenomenon, the effects of which are largely independent of the wills of the participants in a given social formation. That is, the way that most of us, most of the time, conceive of (and structure) our "reality" is predetermined by what are mostly unconscious ideas and opinions that have been inculcated in the process of living in a particular social formation. Whereas the practices resulting from ideology are observable, the experience of ideology itself is an inherently subjective one. It is through ideology that the individual's experience of the external is interpreted (or made sense of) by the individual. In other words, it is a point of articulation between the individual and the social "reality" in which he or she lives. Ideology is what links an individual to his or her "world" in a process of articulation by which an individual interprets (or forms an image of) "reality."[7]

This view of ideology, although not presented in the terms of articulation, is represented in a recent essay by the Mexican historian, Enrique Semo:

> Ideology presents itself to us, in the most immediate manner, as a system of ideas, opinions and customs that provides a sense of cohesion to groups

of people, and at the same time conditions their behavior according to the accepted objectives of a society, class or social organization. The phenomenon of ideology exists as independently of the individual's will as do the relations of production, and it is therefore a fundamental instance of society as a whole. But ideology is also a human representation of the world, and as such it can be the object of study of the theory of knowledge (1987, pp. 2–3; translated by Susan Casal-Sánchez).

This view of ideology, although apparently straightforward, was not accepted as such by Poulantzas. Part of his concern was that such a conception of ideology could only result from an idealist conception and lead to what he saw as the political and theoretical mistake of identifying a class with its political "position." He constructed a conception of ideology that joined it to the workplace (i.e., the "immediate process of production"). Poulantzas contended that ideology is present in the determinations of class to begin with:

> Every objective class place in the production process is necessarily characterized by effects on the structural determination of this class in all aspects, i.e., also by a specific place of this class in the political and ideological relations of the social division of labor (1978, p. 16).

Furthermore, this means that in cases where there is no developed working class consciousness and "even if it is heavily *contaminated by bourgeois ideology,* its economic existence is still expressed in certain specific material politico-*ideological* practices, which burst through its bourgeois 'discourse'; this is what Lenin designated . . . class instinct" (1978, p. 17; emphasis added).

Poulantzas did away "with a whole conception of *ideology* as a 'system of ideas' or a coherent 'discourse,' and [understood] it as an ensemble of material practices. This gives the lie to all those ideologies arguing the 'integration' of the working class, and ultimately it means only one thing: there is no need for there to be 'class consciousness' or autonomous political organizations for the class struggle to take place, and to take place in every domain of social reality" (1978, p. 17).

Poulantzas criticized Lukàcs' notion of "consciousness" (which I equate with ideology in the sense of a system of ideas bounded by class) and the logically subsequent notion of class-in-itself distinguished from class-for-itself. Class antagonism is inherent in the structural determination of class. If there is not structural antagonism (i.e., an opposition determined in the production process) we are not talking about classes. The degree to which social agents are conscious of this antagonism (as antagonism) is irrelevant to the structural determination of class. (Although, he suggests that "consciousness" of the antagonism is inevitable as workers are confronted by the *political* relations of domination and subordination.) This class consciousness is repressed in the normal reproduction of the social relations of production at both the political level and the ideological level.

Poulantzas provided his primary example of what he meant by political and ideological relations of domination and subordination in the analysis of the "new petty bourgeoisie." Within the social division of labor, the supervisor or manager functions to reproduce the subordination of the workers to the capitalist. That is, in the production process, the economic conditions for the extraction of surplus value are enforced, carried out, and continued through the (political) power of the supervisor over the worker.

At the ideological level, Poulantzas referred to the ideological practices that form and directly result in the ideological conditions for the reproduction of relations of production in the workplace (the "immediate process of production") by legitimating the authority of the supervisor. In a capitalist social formation this process involves the alienation of "knowledge" of the techniques of production (including the organization of production) from the direct producer and the reapplication of this "knowledge" as a force of capital against the worker. The class place that performs the function of this reapplication of "knowledge" is marked apart from the working class by the corresponding division between mental and manual labor. Engineers and technicians perform the "technological application of science under the sign of the dominant ideology, which they materialize even in their 'scientific' work; they are thus supports of the reproduction of ideological relations actually within the process of material production" (1978, p. 237). This point of the "social" productive forces of labor being turned against labor as a "productive power of capital" was described by Marx:

> [The development of the social productive forces of labor] takes the form of the *productive power of capital*. It does not appear as the productive power of labor, or even of that part of it that is identical with capital. And least of all does it appear as the productive power either of the individual worker or of the workers joined together in the process of production. The mystification implicit in the relations of capital as a whole is greatly intensified here . . . (*Results of the Immediate Process of Production;* in Appendix 1977, p. 1025).

Poulantzas expounded upon the process of the "mystification" that results in the ideological domination of the worker in the workplace:

> [The] technological applications of science are in the direct service of capitalist production, in so far as they serve the development of capitalist productive forces, since the productive forces only exist dominated by the relations of production. These applications are thus interwoven with ideological practices corresponding to the dominant ideology (1978, p. 236).

Further, there is where Poulantzas applies the notion of making use of political and ideological domination within the immediate process of production as the determination of class place:

> [The] work of technological application of science takes place under the sign of the dominant ideology, which [engineers and technicians] materialize even in their "scientific" work; they are thus supports of the reproduction of ideological relations actually within the process of material production. Their role in the reproduction, by way of the technological application of science, takes the particular form under capitalism of a division between mental and manual labor, which expresses the ideological conditions of the capitalist production process (1978, p. 237).

The white collar "expert" appears to control the "secret knowledge" of the production process. Also, in a more general sense (i.e., toward a system-of-ideas sense of ideology), the idea of the "expert" itself is a part of the dominant ideology in capitalist social formations that workers are not capable of organizing in, or directing, the production process themselves.

Contrary to what might be expected, the delineation of a "new petty bourgeoisie" cannot be reduced to simply a matter of the use of mental labor as opposed to physical labor. Rather, the "mental labor" to which Poulantzas refers is the control of the "know-how" of the "sciences" and "technologies" that is in turn shaped by the organization of the production process (to the advantage of the extraction of surplus value from the direct producer—i.e., the relations of production shape the organization of the production process). It should also be noted that there is a close relationship or articulation between the ideological and the political elements in the production process. As mentioned above, the ideological element (and this is part of what constitutes it as being "ideological") grants legitimacy to the "political" authority of the supervisor. In fact, as Poulantzas noted, it is often true that the same social agent simultaneously occupies an ideological and political place of domination in the production process.

One further point needs to be drawn out here. The analysis of the ideological relations of dominance is, after all, Poulantzas' explanation of the presence and reproduction of the "dominant ideology" in the immediate process of production itself. That is, the site of the reproduction of ideology in a capitalist mode of production is within production and not externally in the form of an "ideological state apparatus" (discussed below). This relationship to the dominant ideology is inherent for Poulantzas: "There is no such thing as a purely technological application of science; every such application is constitutively bound up with the materialization of the dominant ideology in the form of practical knowledge of various kinds" (1978, p. 238).

The idea here of the relationship between "dominant ideology" and class relations of ideological domination and subordination leads to the question of how could such an explanation of the articulation between the production process explain change or explain the notion of latent class ideology that "bursts" out in the "conjuncture." Poulantzas insisted that Lukàcs' idea of "class consciousness" making for a "class-for-itself" (from a class-in-itself) was wrong, because it results from an idealist position that equates class (and class struggle) not with the structure resulting from the process of production, but in the adoption of a "consciousness" or ideology from nowhere but the ideal realm. However, his position meant that Poulantzas needed to provide an explanation for the emergence of new ideologies. That is, as ideology for Poulantzas is grounded within the process of the material relations of production, how can he account for the development of an ideology in opposition to a dominant "ideology" of which an occupant may be "contaminated?"

Another related potential objection here is that Poulantzas failed to provide a satisfying explanation for the psychology of ideology. In his concern to base ideology (inescapably a mental phenomenon) in material practices and so avoid an idealist ontology, he evaded the problem of explaining the mental articulation of the social agent with the class place he or she occupies. One response to this objection is that Poulantzas was explaining the reproduction of class division in the immediate process of production. That is, the problem that Poulantzas set for himself was how to explain why the social agents who perform the reapplication of the knowledge to the production process are thus performing as agents of capital (without being capitalists themselves) and, as such, are apart from the working class (from whom the "knowledge" was appropriated).

Poulantzas demonstrated how the division of mental labor from manual labor (the extraction of the knowledge of the production process from the process itself as found in the capitalist mode of production) is the result of (and results in) an ideologically based class division. The notion of "dominant ideology" and the problem of the mental articulation of that ideology is related to this process of social division, but the problem of explaining this structural process is distinct from the problem of explaining articulation of the individual and the dominant ideology. This is to say, though, that Poulantzas did indeed leave the problem of explaining, for example, exactly why the particular social agent (e.g., an engineer) should individually support or hold an ideology that happens to result in his or her own class place being structurally separate from the place of a social agent of the working class. Put another way, whereas this explanation for a structural division of classes helps to explain the ideological and political domination of the working class in the production process, it leaves unanswered the question of how this division results (or should result) in a difference of "class position."

Clearly, though, Poulantzas is correct to point out that the manager in a capitalist social formation acts on behalf—or exercises the power—of the capitalist within the immediate process of production as a matter of course. This does not necessarily mean that the particular social agents who occupy these places in a capitalist social formation would be any more tied to supporting the capitalist organization of production that their "mental" labor is used to promote than a social agent who occupies a place in the working class would be tied to support the capitalist mode of production that his "manual" labor is also used to promote.[8]

Probably the best response that we can obtain from Poulantzas is that he is concerned with the delineation of "class place" not "class position." (And, in terms of class position, the manager qua capitalist manager is antithetical to an alliance with workers.) As Poulantzas points out, he is concerned to answer those social theorists who would confuse or equate class position (political stance of a class) with class place (structural determination). For example, a "national bourgeoisie" may ally itself in some conjuncture with the working class of a given social formation. That political position does not turn that national bourgeoisie into a working class "for itself." And, on the flip side, a working class is a working class regardless of whether it has demonstrated awareness (e.g., in the form of political organization) of itself as such.

To draw out this point even more, in the event of a socialist revolution, it would be (or should be) true that a socialist social formation would not contain the division that results from technology or science being used on behalf of capital. The engineer or the "management scientist" (and the employment of their techniques in a way that results in domination of the worker) would not exist separate from the working class because, by definition, this knowledge that is alienated from the working class in a capitalist social formation would no longer be so alienated.

How does an ideology come about that would make the "knowledge" of the manager in a socialist formation a reflection of socialist ideology? Poulantzas responded to this question at two levels. First, Poulantzas indicated that, even when heavily "contaminated" with bourgeois ideology, "specific material politico-ideological practices will burst through" within the immediate production process. That is, Poulantzas indicated, albeit without the same structural analysis that he gives to the counterforces, that the legitimacy of the supervisor to exercise authority will be challenged as an outcome of the structural opposition that marks the social division of classes in the process of production. At another, nonstructural level, "class consciousness and autonomous political organization . . . constitute the conditions for the intervention of the classes as social forces" (1978, p. 17). By the very fact that he places ideological and political relations into the "base" of material practices, Poulantzas' conception of mode of production insists upon the notion of a dialectical, interrelational theory of change where change at any level logically involves all elements of the given mode of production.

Another problem in the Poulantzian account of class structure is how to designate the class place of those social agents whose activities are not directly related to the immediate process of production. That is, whereas the supervisor's place is marked by its political domination of the working class and the place of the engineer is marked by the ideological domination of the working class, how do we designate the class place of, say, the teacher (whose activity apparently takes place outside the immediate process of production)? The answer here seems to be that such a place is marked by the ideological domination of the working class in that the "knowledge" purveyed by most teachers maintains domination of the worker for the benefit of the reproduction of conditions for capitalism. It would seem, however, that the concept of the immediate process of production would have to expand to include the school—where workers and managers are trained.[9] That is, the teacher, like the engineer, is involved in the manipulation of knowledge on behalf of the capitalist.

In a recent work (1987), Stephen Resnick and Richard Wolff attempt to do away with this distinction between reproduction of ideology within and without the immediate process of production in a capitalist mode of production by offering the notion of "subsumed classes" as a class "position" (in the Poulantzian sense of "place") that is distinguished by its participation in the production *and distribution process* that is neither that of direct producer or of direct expropriator. One subsumed class place, according to Resnick and Wolff, is that which is involved in the reproduction of ideology. Resnick and Wolff consider this possibility explicitly:

> The subsumed class of directors of the state apparatus often provides, for example, free public education and free public cultural programs. This involves the design and dissemination of concepts of justice, society,

work, individuality, and so forth. These concepts function in people's minds as means to construct and construe their life experiences. Belief in and thinking by means of specific conceptual frameworks are cultural conditions of existence of the capitalist fundamental class process (1987, p. 130).

Resnick and Wolff include—indeed, initially define—a subsumed class position in terms of its position as recipient or distributor of surplus value. I think it is better to maintain a definition of class place that locates it in the production side of the production and reproduction process. That is, it is the way that the particular class performs to allow or maximize the conditions for the extraction of surplus value that should be used to analyze the particular role of the given "subsumed class." To begin speaking in terms of the other side of the production process—the distribution process—would leave us with a vague analysis that would designate class place on the basis of income of those not directly exploited. It would certainly lead us out of relations of production (and corresponding relations of domination at the political and ideological levels).

A logical result here for Poulantzas' argument is that we need to consider all ideological practices—unless they are in either reactionary or revolutionary opposition—to be within the immediate process of production. That is, Poulantzas' argument is forced to the contention that the state itself, for example, becomes a part of the immediate process of production. In the application to the Bolivian case, the problem of what is internal and what is external to the "immediate process" of production is obviated by the fact that we are dealing with a noncapitalist mode of production. In a noncapitalist mode of production (as discussed below) ideological practices may well be conceived to stand outside the immediate process of production in the sense that they can determine the process of production. That is, the actual process of commodity production is not logically prior to ideological practices in the overall process of the reproduction of the given social formation.

APPLICATION TO BOLIVIA

The importance of the above discussion on structural determination of political position to the Bolivian case results from the application of this structural argument to an explanation of the political *position* (as well as place) of the intermediary class,[10] which is determined in the structural articulation of the noncapitalist with the capitalist mode of production. Methodologically, I use the political position of the intermediate agent as an indication of structural determination.

That is, the social agent whose loyalty is indigenous is an agent whose class determination results from an ideological element of the indigenous side of the social formation. The effect of this is that as a "supervisor" this social agent is in opposition to the capitalist side and "supervises" in the name of the indigenous population and not in the name of those of the capitalist side.

The history of Bolivia is marked by a constant struggle at the political level between agents of the two modes of production. Using the theory outlined above, I present that political struggle in terms of the ideological determination of the class place of the social agents whose role in the social formation is the political domination of the peasantry of the indigenous (or noncapitalist) mode of production. The question of the "loyalty" of the social agent becomes more important in cases such as that of Bolivia, where two ideological conditions effectively competed for the "loyalty" of the social agent and, by extension, the determination of class position of, for example, the *kuraka* during the period of Spanish colonialism. For example, this loyalty, viewed in structural terms, helps to explain the maintenance or loss of political authority by the *kuraka* vis-a-vis the indigenous communities.

Another point from the discussion above on the Poulantzas theory of class and ideology relates to the Bolivian situation in terms of how the ideological relations found in the process of production in the capitalist side of the Bolivian social formation affect (or fail to affect) the dominant ideology of the participant or "social agent" who comes to the workplace already "contaminated" with the ideology of the indigenous side (which is reproduced in the material practices of the relations of production of the indigenous side). In the Bolivian situation we also return to the question of whether capitalism generally has developed to a point in the "formal subsumption" of labor to the extent that "knowledge" can be alienated. Certainly, in the indigenous *campo* it had not.

DOMINANT, PREEXISTING, AND NEW IDEOLOGIES

Poulantzas contended that political and ideological social relations are manifested in the practices of the state apparatuses as well as the economic apparatus (1978, p. 25). This would mean that the "dominant ideology" in a capitalist social formation is marked by the fact that its "practices" reflect and hence act to support—legitimate—the conditions for the reproduction of capital. Existing in practices external to the immediate process of production, the mechanisms or apparatuses for maintaining the unity and cohesion of a social formation can be found in the practices and doctrines of religion, education, mass media, political parties, the family, the Boy Scouts, and so forth, which act to "sanction class domination and in this way reproduce [class] relations" (Poulantzas 1978, p. 25). Using Althusser's "idea" (as indicated in his "practice" of writing), I refer to these mechanisms as the "ideological state apparatuses."[11]

If it is true that the practices of these apparatuses reflect and implicitly justify the correctness of the given social relations of production and the consequent power of the ruling class directly or indirectly, it is also true that contradictions in the social relations of production should be reflected in changing (or conflicting) ideological practices. For example, as capitalism developed in Europe, market relations in property and labor (or the move to labor power as property) made feudal ideologies that justified strict hierarchies and intergenerational mutual obligations cumbersome to the emerging bourgeoisie. New ideologies (e.g., protestantism, liberalism) conducive to justifying and explaining capitalist social relations of production emerged and predominated in Europe. However, with the development of capitalism, the system of ideas that had developed in the feudal period (and the apparatuses that practiced those ideas) did not suddenly vanish. An examination of the various capitalist social formations of Europe would need to take into account the accommodations (or articulations) these precapitalist apparatuses formed with emerging capitalist relations of production.

Methodologically, then, we should be able to expect ideological practices to change if social relations of production change. Conversely, preexisting ideological apparatuses may be seen to exhibit something of their own "relative autonomy" within the contradictions of changing social relations of production. The Catholic Church is probably a good example here. Predating capitalism as an ideological apparatus, we might be able to view it, at least partially, as a continuation of a feudal state apparatus. Without denying that the Church clearly accommodated emerging capitalism, it also clearly maintained and justified certain class arrangements in capitalist Southern Europe that could be contrasted with developments in Northern Europe, where the reformation aided states (or states aided the reformation) in overthrowing the feudal state apparatus of the Catholic Church, which, in turn, helped the bourgeoisie cast off the effects of ideas that might result in "inefficiencies" in the production process.

Furthermore, this relative autonomy could help us explain the fact that apparatuses could be the sites of the development of new ideas. That is, precisely because apparatuses are external to the immediate production process of new modes of production, those new relations of production cannot, structurally speaking, purify the preexisting apparatus of all its previous ideological practices. An obvious example here would be the changed ideological practices in Latin America, emerging from within a segment of the Catholic Church, and the support those practices gave to revolutionary change in Nicaragua in the 1980s.[12]

The role of human agency also can be seen to enter here. Using Althusser's notion of theoretical practice, the dominant ideology can be escaped (to various degrees) and the invisible (unconscious)[13] relations of ideological dominance can be revealed and examined at the individual level in the terms of theoretical analysis.[14] In this process, structures that were once opaque (or mystifying) would reveal themselves as the relations of domination that they are. Further, there is nothing in the "structuralist" view proposed above that would force us to concede that ideas contrary to the "interests" of the dominant class cannot exist within the "system of ideas." First, as discussed above, some ideological apparatuses are not completely reflective of the dominant mode's relations of production. Second, the fact that dominant ideology may be viewed as functioning generally to the benefit of the dominant class does not necessarily make the ideology less mystifying to the dominant class than it is to a dominated class. As Semo points out (1987, pp. 2–3), occupants of the bourgeoisie may honestly believe that the values they hold as good are good for everyone (i.e., serve the interests of everyone). This very universalization of values results in contradictions that wait to be discovered. That is, ideas within the dominant ideology may serve as a basis for the transformation of dominated classes as occupants of those class places are confronted with the economic and political "reality" of their dominated places in the social relations of production. This, in turn, could be one basis for (and the reflection of) "class ideology" and class struggle.

Real decisions and choices can be made at the individual level. But, decisions regarding individual action in the "world" are limited by the unconscious acceptance of ideas that define ones conception of what is, and what is desirable and/or possible. Furthermore, action itself is limited by economic and political "realities," as well as ideological structures in which one lives. As Marx put it in an often quoted passage of the *Eighteenth Brumaire of Louis Bonaparte:* "men make their own history, but they do not make it just as they please; they do not make it under circumstances chosen by themselves, but under circumstances directly encountered, given and transmitted from the past . . ." (1968, p. 97).

PRECONDITIONS FOR THE INTRUSION OF CAPITALISM AND IMMEDIATE AND EXTERNAL PROCESSES OF PRODUCTION

In the examination of noncapitalist social formations, one primary distinguishing characteristic is the use of extraeconomic coercion for the extraction of surplus value from the direct producer. One significant facet of Poulantzas' use of ideological and political elements within the immediate process of production is the recognition of the continuing, though dominated, presence of those factors at the site of production in a capitalist mode. This is not to say that Poulantzas did away with extraeconomic coercion as a distinguishing characteristic of noncapitalist formations. The worker in a capitalist mode of production is separated from the ownership of the means of production and is forced by economic necessity to enter into the capitalist's domain—the production site. Nonetheless, ideological and political factors are performing here. The political authority of the supervisor—an authority to coerce at the site—is still present.

Perhaps somewhat ironically, Poulantzas' analysis shifts the distinguishing characteristic to that of capitalism's double structure of internal ideological and political relations as well as external manifestations (or reflections) of these relations in the reproduction process. That is, the better distinction to be made between a noncapitalist and capitalist mode of production is not the absence of political and ideological processes in the immediate process of production; rather it is the very incorporation (and subordination) of those processes into the direct economic process of the exploitation of labor.

In a noncapitalist mode of production there is no double structure, and there is no distinction to be made between the processes of production that are internal and those that are external to the immediate process:

> The superstructures of kinship, religion, law or the state necessarily enter into the constitutive structure of the mode of production in pre-capitalist social formations. They intervene *directly* in the internal nexus of surplus-extraction, where in capitalist social formations, the first in history to separate the economy as a formally self-contained order, they provide by contrast its "external" preconditions (Anderson 1979, pp. 403–5).

Using the Incan social formation as an example (discussed in Chapter 3), I maintain that there is no reason to distinguish between the immediate process of production and the overall or general process of production (or social reproduction). The gods (or *huacas*) were viewed by the direct producers as being directly involved in the immediate process of production. The gods were carefully addressed by the direct producer because they affected production (e.g., the outcome of the harvest and the health and fertility of the household). The priest controlled the "knowledge" of production (and reproduction) to the extent that the priest determined the method (rituals) of addressing the gods. These same priests, in the name of these gods (and the rituals celebrated around them), provided "legitimacy" to the social relations of production within the social formation. In the Incan social formation the priests were the equivalent of the engineer and "management specialist" in a capitalist social formation. They also fulfilled the equivalent function of a capitalist formation's ISAs by simultaneously providing the "external" grant of legitimacy to the dominant place of the ruling class (i.e., they gave the "amen" to the status quo).

Part of the power of Poulantzas' analysis is that it helps us explain how a capitalist mode of production places its ideological and political reproduction within the economic process of production. An outcome of this is that the state ideological apparatuses do not set the pre-conditions for the reproduction of capitalist relations of production; they either "wither" or survive as reflections of the immediate process of production itself. Whereas, in a noncapitalist social formation, religion, for example, may be directly involved in the production process. The production process itself may even be dominated by religion in the "last instance"; another way of saying that the production process is for the purpose of reproducing the conditions for the existence of this ideology (as a capitalist production process reproduces the conditions for capital).

In a capitalist social formation, certain preexisting ideologies and/or political institutions may be helpful to the development of capitalism, but religion and other ideological apparatuses are decidedly relegated to a role external to the immediate process of production. The possible implications of this are drawn out below.

CONCLUSION

A mode of production, as used in this study, contains three significant processes: political, ideological, and economic. Each of these processes constitutes a possible point of articulation with another mode of production; and methodologically, these points of articulation are the focuses of this analysis. At the economic level, this articulation can be seen in the form of commodity exchange (markets) and in the use of labor from one mode in the "area" of the other mode. During the colonial period, for example, we find that the Spanish made use of indigenous labor power in the mines of Potosí. However, though the Spanish directed this labor to their own ends, they used a preexisting indigenous labor arrangement or relation known as the *mit'a*.

At the political and ideological levels, an extension of Poulantzas' analysis allows us to view the existence of a particular class place as a result of the process of the reproduction of the articulation at the political and ideological of the two modes at those levels. Further, as a result of the fact that in a noncapitalist mode of production the ideological and political processes are not dominated by (or determined within) the immediate processes of production (the economic element), the ideology of the noncapitalist modes of production may be said to be in an open form. Whereas in a capitalist mode of production ideology is bound to the immediate process of production, in a noncapitalist mode of production ideology is unbound. Among other things, this characteristic should alert us to the structural underpinning of the arguments made by representatives of the current *katarista* movement in Bolivia.

One possible implication, taken up in Chapter 6, is that the reproduction of the *indígena* noncapitalist-oriented ideology in Bolivia is not dependent upon a complete continuation of indigenous social relations—relating to reciprocity, and sacred consideration of the earth. *Indígenas* who entered class places within the capitalist mode of production could be resistant to the ideological demands of those class places. Further, whereas certain political and ideological arrangements may be conducive to the intrusion and internal development of capitalist relations of production, the ideology of the indigenous population in Bolivia was being used in the 1970s and 1980s by a growing *indigenista* movement as political justification to resist capitalist relations of production and exploitation.

In the Bolivian situation we have a case in which there are two distinct modes of production. In the process of the indigenous mode's articulation with the tributary/capitalist side of the social formation, the colonial and Bolivian state was structurally required to make use of existing indigenous leadership places to act as intermediary between themselves and the indigenous direct producers. This was a symptom of the fact that the Spanish did not break up indigenous relations of production. Even in the use of indigenous labor the Spanish made use of the indigenous method of labor tribute and, thus, did not bring indigenous labor into capitalist relations of production.[15]

The next chapter discusses the argument that this articulation of tributary/capitalist with the noncapitalist mode created a class place that was occupied by the rough equivalent of the new petty bourgeoisie. In this case, the class place of the "intermediary" class was structured in the processes of articulation between the two modes; not within the process of production of either mode. Nonetheless, this intermediary class place was structured by the ideological and political processes necessary to the reproduction of the social formation. Inevitable contradiction arose from the fact that the tributary/capitalist side relied upon this class to dominate the indigenous population through political and economic relations (in the name of the ruling class on the capitalist side). One way to solve this structural contradiction from the capitalist point of view was to eliminate the *kuraka* (and equivalent), get directly at the indigenous population, and—ideally—force it into capitalist relations of production. The taking of indigenous community land and the construction of the hacienda system in the late 1800s was one way to attempt this. One result was a massive indigenous rebellion led by Pablo Zárate Willka at the turn of the twentieth century. Another result was the participation of the *campesinado* in the revolution of 1952 and the agrarian reform of 1953.

NOTES

1. Poulantzas uses the term "place" to refer to the concept of a structural space that is occupied by individuals (social agents). Class "places" compose classes, not the individuals who happen to occupy that place. However, to the extent that class place carries an ideological determination, an occupant of a class place is bounded by those determinations. I agree with Poulantzas's notion that a place is mutually determined (or structured) by the formation's economic, political, and ideological structures. To occupy a "place" is to be affected in action by the structural demands of that "place." Resnick and Wolff (1987), among others, have a similar notion of "place." (Resnick and Wolff use the word "position" to refer to the structured "place." Poulantzas uses the word "position" to indicate the political stance, or alliances, that a class makes in a "conjuncture.") One important distinction between Resnick and Wolff and Poulantzas in the notion of "place/position" is that Resnick and Wolff do not make use of the notion of ideological and political structures determining class "place/position," rather, they make a distinction between "fundamental" and "subsumed" classes. Fundamental classes are the positions that fall into the primary economic categories—direct producer and direct exploiter—in the process of the extraction of surplus value. Subsumed classes are composed of those positions that (separately) reproduce ideological and political structures, which act to support the activities of the fundamental classes. Resnick and Wolff are then able to handle the problematic of "intermediary" class positions by explicating those class positions as subsumed class positions (see Resnick and Wolff 1987, pp. 118–19).

2. This term indicates the sense of its intermediate location and mediating political function between two modes; not in the sense of "middle class."

3. Reference here is to Althusser's concept of "theoretical practice," as I understand it. See *Reading Capital*, Verso edition, with Brewster's glossary.

4. I do assign the label "indigenous mode of production" to the mode of production of the "noncapitalist" processes of the Bolivian social formation. However, I do not claim, and neither would it be meaningful to claim, that this is somehow a newly discovered mode of production. Labels cannot be discovered; processes can be examined in the interest of explaining historical outcomes.

5. Although not stating it quite so boldly, Eric Wolf gives something of a similar view of modes-of-production analysis as an analysis of processes rather than typology in his 1982 work: Modes of productions "are put forth as constructs with which to envisage certain strategic relationships that shape the terms under which human lives are conducted. [The three modes discussed here] are instruments for thinking about the crucial connections built up among the expanding Europeans and the other inhabitants of the globe, so that we may grasp the consequences of these connections" (1982, p. 100).

6. See Wolpe (1980), and Claude Meillasoux takes up this topic of the limits of superexploitation in his book, *Maidens, Meal and Money* (1981).

7. The notion of ideology determining the subjective perceptions of "reality" is readily evidenced by the observations of other social formations by anthropologists. Professor Michael Kearney takes up this issue in his book, *World View:* "From a purely physical point of view we can assume that the phenomenal world is a single continuum of energy and matter in motion. The anthropological study of comparative philosophy [of literate and nonliterate peoples] readily demonstrates that there is no general consensus about the nature of reality. Assumptions about reality vary considerably from one group to another, and at bottom they depend upon and affect the actual perception of it . . . (1984, p. 41).

8. Eric Olin Wright (1978) dismisses the division between mental and manual labor because it is too ambiguous, among other reasons. The heart of the problem here is that the process of the alienation of "knowledge" from the worker is part of the structural condition of the worker. Structurally, then, it makes sense to define those social agents involved in the reapplication of that "knowledge" in its alienated form as involved in a process of production separate from that process of the working class. In contrast, one can as well argue (and Poulantzas did not deny this) that the social agent who is exploited in his or her relation to capital via mental labor is as alienated from the whole production process by his or her separation from manual labor (not to mention the fact that his or her mental labor is subject to the same exploitation in terms of the extraction of surplus value from that social agent's labor power). However, the importance of the process of alienating "knowledge" and reconstructing it as a force of capital is enough to make that "place" that carries out this function (of capital) structurally separate from the place of the direct producer. As explained in the text, the problem here is the distinction between class place and class "position."

9. Again, as in the case of the manager, the process of reproduction—the practice of the apparatus—determines the actions of the teacher. Most business management teachers in an MBA program, advertised as something to help the student gain a promotion, will not bother their students with talk of overthrowing capitalist relations of production.

10. The term "intermediary class" is explained in more detail in Chapter 2.

11. See his essay *Ideology and the State,* originally published in 1970, for a definition and discussion of the "ISAs." Some of the basic points are that ISAs are, in effect, the institutional embodiments of various regions of the dominant ideology. Althusser insisted on the notion that ideology is in the "practice" of the ideology (i.e., not in the "idea" of the ideology). The ISA is the location of the particular "practice." It is an ideological state apparatus because, one, its role is to legitimate the given social relations of production. (The "Repressive State Apparatuses" are only used against the individuals who somehow escape becoming the "subject" of, or finding their reflection in, the ISAs.) And, two, the concept of civil society being in the realm of the "State" makes civil institutions State institutions. In this essay, Althusser makes the point that the ISA does not originate the dominant ideology, and to understand ideology it must be seen from the "point of view" of the production process; which is what Poulantzas is up to in his 1978 work.

12. Clearly, there are some complicated issues here that I cannot do justice to in a few paragraphs. The main idea here for the text is simply to lead into the discussion on preexisting conditions for the intrusion of capitalism (which relates directly to Bolivia). Having said that, I add that revolutions usually entail a complete overthrow of the state,

which includes the state apparatuses. Certainly any practice that "got in the way" could probably be removed through political coercion. That is, the new state would act either to incorporate or repress preexisting apparatuses and their practices. Nonetheless, new states may be weak, revolutions may be incomplete.

13. To clarify further, the ideas contained in an ideology are not the thing that the bearer of the ideology is unconscious of (though some actions or attitudes may indeed be performed without any thought at all—i.e., they are "natural" or "common sense"). Rather, it is the fact that the bearer of the ideology is unconscious of the "fact" that his or her ideas (as justification for behavior or attitudes) are the result of an ideology, which as an entire "system of ideas" serve to dominate the bearer.

14. Such a process would be a matter of making conscious that which is normally unconscious (or making transparent tht which was previously opaque).

15. After the development of wage labor in the mines we can still see evidence of the indigenous population's lack of ideological subsumption into the capitalist side in the practice of "devil" worship (see Taussig 1980, and Platt, in *Fe y pueblo* 1986).

Chapter 3
Original Characteristics of the Indigenous Social Formation and Its Articulation with Capitalism

This chapter covers the periods of the Incan social formation's encounter with Spanish colonialism, the *indígena* rebellions, and the encroachment of the hacienda system into the indigenous communities during the 1800s. The purpose of this historical coverage is to demonstrate the dynamics of the indigenous mode of production as it interacted with the tributary mode[1] brought to the Andes by the Europeans. This demonstration is intended to support the thesis that the modal structure (the political, ideological, and economic elements) of the indigenous mode of production was not eliminated by contact and articulation with the imposed tributary and capitalist mode of production. It is also intended to show that there is a strong historical continuity to the process of the articulation between the two modes. This continuity has made for a predictable struggle at the political level between the two modes that has centered on the class whose "place" was created or determined in that process of intermodal articulation.

An understanding of this intermediary class place, and the major rift or zone of conflict between the two modes of production that it straddles, can be best approached through concepts (discussed in Chapter 2) regarding the concept of "class place" developed by Nicos Poulantzas. Specifically, I use the notion of a class place that is not determined or situated by the economic category of labor surplus expropriation—neither direct expropriator nor provider of directly expropriated surplus value. Rather, this intermediary class can be distinguished by its ideological function as it acted to manipulate the "knowledge" of production to the end of the extraction of surplus value from the class of direct producers. This class place contained both those who manipulated that knowledge (e.g., the priesthood) and the "supervisors" who gained their political authority as "supervisor" through the ideology perpetuated through the priesthood (and other nobility). By using political and ideological criteria (as well as economic) to determine class place, Poulantzas (1978) provided a definition and explanation of the "new petty bourgeoisie" existing in monopoly capitalist formations. By using the same ideological and political criteria, this chapter examines the class structure within the "indigenous mode of production," and demonstrates the impact on that structure brought about in the articulation of the indigenous mode of production with the capitalist mode of production of the Spanish.

The major premise of this chapter is that the stakes of political conflict within Spanish Alto Perú and Bolivia had been (and, as argued in Chapter 5, continued to be) the ideological determination of the class place that functioned (most of the time) to allow the capitalist mode of production to politically dominate the indigenous mode of production. That is, the dominant political struggle, which took place in the space allowed by weak capitalist development vis-à-vis resistant indigenous social structures, had centered, in structural terms, on the issue of which ideology—capitalist mode or indigenous mode—determined the class place of the intermediary class.

CLASS PLACE

Class place is determined in (or is a result of) the process of production. This makes "class place" a derivative of mode of production. A mode of production is the given combination of the ideological, political, and economic processes. How these processes come together is determined or structured within the immediate process of production in a capitalist mode of production and in the overall process of social reproduction in a noncapitalist mode. The historical reality of the social formation, however, involves the articulation of modes of production. The process of articulation, which is involved in the overall reproduction of the given social formation, involves the determination of the equivalent of "class place." However, this equivalent category, unlike Poulantzas' notion of "class place" in a capitalist mode of production, is not created or structured in the immediate process of production. Rather, it is a result of the process of structural articulation.

It should be recalled from the theoretical discussion in Chapter 2 that a capitalist mode of production distinguishes itself from other modes by its double structure, wherein the ideological and political elements of the mode are part of the immediate process of production and therein are subordinated to the economic requirements of capitalist organization. Noncapitalist modes are not characterized by this split into a double structure of immediate process of production versus external or overall process of social reproduction. That is, other kinds of modes (or, more accurately, model processes) do not contain the same structural mechanism for dominating the ideological and political elements of the mode. The implications of this for the Bolivian study is that the ideological elements of the noncapitalist side of the social formation are at something of an advantage in that capitalist relations of production must establish themselves within an environment that is pervaded by the unconfined ideological element of the indigenous mode of production. Given that the ideological element of the indigenous side is not conducive to capitalist relations of production, then the special problem for the capitalist side is how the articulation at the ideological and political level is going to work. Historically, this problem was solved through the simple use of violence, the bought or captured loyalty of the *kuraka* (the indigenous leadership), and the locking of noncapitalist labor relations into the capitalist side through the hacienda system. This chapter argues that the underlying structural situation here is that political domination or coordination of the indigenous side by the capitalist side must account for the ideological element.

I contend in the following analysis of the Bolivian social formation that the ideological and political elements of class determination extend to those areas or "nodal points" (as Poulantzas called them) where one mode of production is joined with another mode of production.[2] Whereas the area of economic articulation may involve the human crossover from one mode to another or the crossover of surplus value from one mode to another in empirically observable terms of seasonal migration or the commodification of products from a noncapitalist mode in the market exchange of the capitalist mode, political and ideological articulation may involve (as it did in Bolivia) the creation of a class structure. This structure is not the direct result of the processes of production of either side; the conditions of its existence are created in the process of the articulation at the political level (which involves the ideological coordination, granting of "legitimacy" to the domination of the one by the other) and the reproduction of the social formation.

This problem should be immediately qualified by the fact that the articulation of a capitalist mode with a noncapitalist mode does not necessarily mean that "political coordination" takes place through the manipulation of the ideological element of the noncapitalist mode. Indeed, probably the typical pattern of the historical encounters between capitalist and noncapitalist social formations is the initial (and long-term) use of the repressive state apparatus. That is, when the conditions do not exist or cannot be manufactured, the dominant class of the dominant mode makes use of simple violence. However, the articulation (and political and economic) domination of noncapitalist modes by capitalist modes has taken place without the constant use of violence. The framework that I propose here (and use to explain Bolivian history) is, in one way, an attempt to explain how a capitalist mode can politically control a noncapitalist mode without the constant use of open repression, and, at the same time, why that political control can be tenuous.

At the economic level the primary argument of this chapter is that the indigenous social arrangement of the *ayllu* was a self-sufficient (self-reproducing) economic and social unit. As successive (though not necessarily continuous) "empires" (or *ayllu*-based ethnic groups) dominated regions of *ayllus* in terms of labor and product extraction, the *ayllus* retained their distinctive, self-sufficient aspects.

THE *AYLLU*

Before the arrival of the Spanish, the *ayllu* was the basic and enduring unit of the organization of agricultural production. As a unit of social organization, the *ayllu* was not specific to the Incan social formation. Rather, the Incas had, as had polities before them, imposed an administrative (extractive) structure upon the preexisting *ayllu* social organization. The individual *ayllus* could be (and at times had been) self-sufficient organizations of social and economic activity. Although the Incan state had organized and coordinated the activities of the *ayllu* units in its jurisdiction for the purpose of the extraction of surplus, the *ayllus* were not broken up by the Incan state.

Heinz Dieterich (1982) classified the *ayllu* as a "gens," or clan organization, which evolved into an hierarchical, class-structured social organization, via the formation of centralized states, by the time of the Inca conquest.[3] However, apparently the internal organization of the *ayllus* remained a largely clanlike structure throughout their articulation with encompassing polities. As agrarian-based, egalitarian communities, the *ayllus* were articulated with the dominant states at economic, ideological, and political nodal points, which historically did little to change the internal social organization of the *ayllu*. To the present, the *ayllu* internal organization has maintained mechanisms for the relatively equal internal distribution of access to land and decisionmaking based largely upon social relations of mutual reciprocity.[4]

Certainly, a large part of the explanation for the long-term maintenance of an internal social coherence of the *ayllu*, despite the empire or confederation building of various ethnic groups, was the lack of trade between or among *ayllus*. The development of a commercial class was never required (or allowed), because a single *ayllu* would locate farming communities within the differing agricultural zones provided by the sharply varying elevations between the high, dry, cold "puna" (or the "altiplano") and the fertile, tropical "yungas" and lower Andean valleys. The movement of products from one zone to the other was a matter of administration rather than commerce.

INCAN SOCIAL FORMATION

In terms of technology or forces of production, the Incan social formation was not at the per capital productive capacity of the Europeans: "The tools of the broader production process were essentially limited to a neolithic technical level" (Dieterich 1982, p. 114). The lack of the iron plow, wheel, or draft animal is a characteristic we would expect to be associated with preponderantly agrarian societies.[5] The level of the forces of production may be viewed, however, as symptomatic of an agrarian-based society that was well organized in terms of the coordination of human labor by the state structure.

Regardless of the level of technology, the Incan social formation used a detailed system of accounting known as the *quipus,* which permitted the systematic exploitation of labor. The Incan state built elaborate and efficient transportation and communication systems that were more sophisticated than those systems found in Europe. Productivity of the land was increased by means of such intensive improvement projects as the construction of terraced fields and irrigation systems, and the use of fertilizers, along with crop domestication (potato, oca, etc.). Therefore, despite the low level of technical development, Inca agriculture not only produced a continuous and secure supply of subsistence products for the rural population and urban masses, but also created a large economic surplus (Dieterich 1982, p. 114).

Although the time span has been questioned by some skeptical historians,[6] the Incan state itself apparently emerged (from its original Cuzco base) in 1438, less than 100 years before the 1532 invasion led by Pizarro. As John Murra points out, the archeological evidence indicates that the Incas had the benefit of an inheritance of the knowledge of statecraft from centuries of previous Andean monarchs. "Wari, Chimu, Tiwanaku—all were pre-Inca states. . . . How to incorporate and then govern disparate linguistic and ethnic groups was part of the political repertoire of thousands of local Andean lords well before A.D. 1000" (1986, p. 49). This skill developed from the need of local Andean (puna-based) lords to extend their jurisdiction to the valley regions where agricultural products could be garnered that enhanced the otherwise spare diet of any group attempting to live from altiplano agriculture. Significantly, there is no evidence that trade or commerce had developed between the high, arid altiplano and the areas of the fertile hillsides and valleys of the tropical eastern Andes. Resource extraction from the valleys for the "nucleus" or original community on the altiplano was through the extra-economic control of the "outlier" farming communities (of the same kin group as that of the nucleus community) and the trafficking of products to the highland community.

Murra's contention that the long-distance extension of effective resource control led to skill in long-distance political control is well taken. Yet, it should be noted that the special geography of the Andes probably allowed many *ayllus* to divide themselves into at least three levels (elevations) of production on a single mountain slope and adjacent valley—the community of farmers at each level interrelated ideologically and organically to the members of the other communities.[7] The significant factor here is that trade— conducted by individuals who are motivated by price differentials—did not develop. Rather, the extra-economic coercion of the *ayllu* extended to the long-distance extraction and transportation of agricultural and (some mineral) products.

In the century or so preceding the expansion of the Inca, these economic and political arrangements were breaking down in the face of conflicting claims of multiethnic communities to the resources of the lower elevations. Archaeologists describe this period as the "Late Intermediate." Local traditions reasserted themselves after the collapse of the earlier Tiwanaku-Wari integration. The *ayllus* re-emerged as independently sovereign entities. The largest highland polities recorded by the oral tradition were of the order of 20,000 to 30,000 households, and Murra speculates that around 1400 the Inca population at Cuzco was of a comparable size. When the Incan expansion began, the drive was probably fueled by what they perceived as a need for new subjects and new productive energies (Murra 1986, p. 50).

Rapid expansion was made possible by the Inca's strategy of not waiting to consolidate each step of the expansion. Murra argues that the initial aim of the Inca did not require thorough control of every pocket and valley. "The striking force could move swiftly, leapfrogging over nuclei of resistance, particularly as [they did not face universal resistance]" (1986, p. 51). Domination of the Inca over the conquered ethnic groups was cemented in part through the exchange of wives. Each local chieftain or *kuraka*[8] was expected to take as his principal wife a woman of the Inca's[9] lineage. The sons born of the principal wife were then to inherit their father's estate and political position. In turn, the Inca accepted into his harem a woman of the conquered ruler's lineage.[10]

The position of the *kuraka* was of obvious importance to the maintenance of stable Incan control of the *ayllus*. If the system of intermarriage established by the Inca went as planned, the *kuraka* at the local level, after one generation following incorporation into the Incan empire, would be a blood descendant of the Incan ruling family. Being the grandson of an Incan ruler was important because of the ideology promulgated by Incan religion that the Incas (rulers) were descendants of the sun. Whether a blood descendant or not, the class place of the *kuraka* was determined at the area of ideological and political articulation between the Inca and the *ayllu*.

It was also at that time an area of political struggle. As the Inca attempted to use the *kuraka* as a mechanism for locking in administrative (political) control of the subject *ayllus,* he needed *kurakas* who, at the ideological level, were loyal to him and thus enforced the administrative (political) mechanism for the extraction of surplus value from the *ayllus*. However, this ideological domination was not secure enough to maintain a reliable "legitimacy" or basis for political authority all the time. According to Murra, oral tradition reported "rapid incorporation in Tawantinsuyu as frequently as the urgent need to reconquer, to defeat again and again, ethnic groups listed as already inside the porous frontier" (1986, p. 52). This continuous need to reconquer meant that ideological control (implemented through religion) was not sufficient for maintaining political authority. The repressive state apparatus was apparently as necessary as the use of the ideological state apparatus.

One effect of this need for repression was the heavy conscription of the *ayllu* population for service as soldiers. The initial use of the *mit'a* for the provision of soliders (within a system of rotation among other obligations) made use of and fortified the *ayllu* social arrangement. That is, the use of the *ayllu* in this way by the Incan state was a type of articulation between the dominant polity and local mode of production that reinforced rather than broke down the organization of the local mode of production. However, the occupation of soldier became a specialized function and was separated from the rotation system of the *mit'a* in which all *ayllus* were required to participate.

Murra takes up the argument that the use of the *mit'a* for the Incan state's requirement of soldiers came to be viewed by Cuzco as inefficient: "The army was increasingly fighting far from the soldier's home base; the countryside was unfamiliar; rotation, lineage after lineage, was difficult to enforce. The Inca chose a solution by which certain ethnic groups were . . . excused from any other duties and assigned to provide only fighting men, recruited according to criteria of bravery that ignored *mit'a* rotation" (1986, pp. 53–54). In effect, the occupation of soldier moved away from an occupation as one among many performed by the direct producers to the specialized function of the organized manipulation of violence. Such an activity would require its own application of "knowledge"—the organization of violence. The soldiers of the Inca would also, of course, have to retain an ideology that made them loyal to the Inca. As such, the class place of the soldier—like that of the *kuraka* and priest—became an intermediary class place.

The point made by Murra from the specialized use of the soldier (i.e., exclusive use of the most loyal ethnic groups and disregarding the traditional labor extraction of the *mit'a* for this purpose) is that Cuzco began a process of breaking up the self-sufficiency and, thus, the long-term distinctiveness of an ethnic group apart from the social formation of the Incan Empire. The idea here is that the overarching Incan state was becoming a mechanism for the breakdown of provincial or *ayllu* communities. That is, intervening barriers among *ayllus* would break down as populations took on specialized functions in the social formation formed by the political and economic articulation of the Incan state with the *ayllu*. The best but probably only example was that of military specialization. Even in this case, though, the military burden was taken on as an ethnic group, as opposed to the best soldiers (or able-bodied) from each community. Thus even in this specialized function, which would detract from self-sufficiency as they became a new intermediary class, they maintained a self-awareness as an ethnically distinct group. Indeed, they present themselves to the Spanish historians as: "We are the four nations, the Charcas and Caracaras and Chuis and Chichas. . . . We have been soldiers since the time of the ingas (sic), called Inga Yupangui, and Topa Inga, and Guaina Capac. . . . We were only soldiers [excused from all other forms of tribute]" ("El memorial de Charcas," Espinoza Sorano [1582] 1969, p. 24; cited in Murra 1986, p. 54). The ethnic identity was proudly proclaimed first.

The breakup of the *ayllu* by the Incan state was further inhibited by the fact that the state did not allow individuals to leave the *ayllu* of origin of their own initiative. In order to guarantee the accuracy of the statistical calculations, which were of vital importance to the functioning of the entire productive and distributive system, the dominant Incan ruling class instituted a form of bondage that prohibited the *ayllu* members from leaving the *ayllu* in which they were registered (Dieterich 1982, p. 117). Dieterich argues further that the articulation established between the state and the *ayllu* contributed to its continuation, not its dissolution:

> It is a unique form in that the relation of exploitation is between the state and the entire community and is carried out while conserving the clan system and without altering its traditional structures, such as, for example, the collective possession of the land, the collective system of labor and its ceremonial character (1982, p. 118).

During the period of Incan dominance, the viability of the *ayllu* (as a unit) did not become dependent on the Incan state. Regardless of the merits of Murra's point regarding the possible incipient breakup of the *ayllu* within the Incan social formation, such a process, if it did begin, was interrupted by the arrival of the Spanish in 1532. The *ayllu* was quite capable of surviving the destruction of the Incan state by the Spanish.

KNOWLEDGE AND CLASS

The nobility reproduced itself—its dominant class place—by monopolizing the "knowledge" of the techniques of the organization of production and reproduction of the social formation. The nobility—including the priesthood—were "taught the secrets of the quipus [record keeping through the use of knots], astrology, religion, philosophy, and laws" (Dieterich 1982, p. 119). The exclusivity of the "secret knowledge" of the Incan social formation is further supported in a statement reportedly made by one of the Incan rulers, Túpac Inca Yupanqui:

> It is not permissible to teach plebeian children about the sciences, which pertain to the noble people and no one else; because as lower people they should not become proud and arrogant and (never) deprecate the republic; for them it is enough to understand the offices of their parents; leading and governing is not for plebeians, to entrust such roles to common people is an affront to the office and to the republic (Prescott 1967, p. 98; cited in Dieterich 1982, p. 120).

The priesthood and other nobility of the Incas reproduced class relations in their social formation both through the promulgation of the idea that they and the ruler were superior to the direct producers and by keeping to themselves that "secret knowledge" of the reproduction of the social formation.[11] That is, the reproduction of the class order of the Incan social formation depended upon certain beliefs (as well as physical violence). Those beliefs were maintained through the operation of ideology at two levels.

First, at one level, we can say that the "knowledge" of the ruling class, its priesthood, and bureaucracy was ideological in terms of content because that "knowledge" was used to organize and justify productive activity for the benefit of a particular interest. That is, rather than the "objective truth" (which it was presented as, no doubt, to most direct producers), the "knowledge" of the ruling class was a set of beliefs that promoted the interests of the Inca. To draw this point out somewhat (and show the connection to Poulantzas' analysis), the "knowledge" of the Incan priest was the equivalent of the knowledge of a corporate manager in a monopoly capitalist social formation. The priest's knowledge of the gods and nature (presented as objective truth) served to justify to the direct producer his or her subordination to the dominant class in much the same way that the manager's knowledge of "good" business organization (presented as "good for everyone"—i.e., serving a universal interest) serves to justify to the worker his or her subordination to the capitalist. Ideology is operating here at a second level. In both cases the "knowledge" is viewed as being "knowledge" (and not as ideology). The fact that the holder of the "knowledge" should be respected as an "expert" or as "divinely inspired" is itself an example of how the social formation relied upon ideology at a second level. That is, the ritual and religion practiced by the population enforced their belief in the correctness of the social order.

The fact that religion and the priesthood played an essential role in the domination of the Incas over the conquered *ayllus* is noted by Dieterich:

> A series of measures . . . strengthened and perpetuated by the concentration and consolidation of the effective military, economic, and political power within a centralized state apparatus, and by the religious legitimation of a powerful state church, headed by the Inca himself. "*The state and the church were completely identified with each other; religion and politics were based on the same principles and authority. The religious was resolved in the social*" (Mariátegui 1972, p. 164; cited in Dieterich, p. 120, my emphasis).

It is this process involving the manipulation of "knowledge" for the purposes of reproducing the Incan social formation and exploiting the direct producers that places this priesthood into the category used by Poulantzas to determine the "new petty bourgeoisie." Since "bourgeoisie" implies the development of capitalism, the term for this class as used here will simply be "intermediary" class. Other than its determination at the political and ideological level, this class can also be characterized by its mediating function within the Incan social formation. By manipulating ideology to link the direct producers of the *ayllus* to the Incan ruling class, the priesthood and the *kurakas* (the legitimacy of whose actions on behalf of the Inca depended upon the "knowledge" of the priesthood) occupied intermediary class places.

During Spanish colonization and the Bolivian social formation the occupants of this intermediary class functioned to link (and sometimes to delink) the direct producer to the new ruling classes.

SPANISH COLONIZATION

As Nathan Wachtel (1977) put it, the indigenous population of the Andes discovered Europe for the first time in the persons of the few hundred Spaniards who conquered them. Francisco Pizarro and his band of soldiers came upon the Incan empire when it was experiencing a civil war brought about through a leadership transition struggle between two sons of the previous Inca. Huascar, who was born of the union of the previous Inca with the primary wife, and another son, Altahuallpa, born of a union with a secondary wife, both claimed the throne. In 1533 Altahuallpa had just captured Huascar, but "legitimist" armies were still resisting him in the region of Cuzco. It was at this time that the Spanish arrived.

Indian reactions to the invaders seem to have been determined by allegiance to one or other of the warring factions. The forces loyal to Huascar initially perceived Pizarro as an aid from the gods to defend the claim of Huascar to the throne. The *indígenas* were disabused of this notion after witnessing the behavior of the Spaniards. However, this at least meant that Pizarro was able to advance without being attacked by the Huascar forces, and the forces of Altahuallpa may have been unable to attack Pizarro for fear of Huascar's forces. In any case, Altahuallpa would not have expected the possibility of reinforcement of Pizarro's band from the Pacific coast and he probably did not perceive the small numbers with Pizarro as a serious military threat. At a meeting between Pizarro and Altahuallpa in Cajamarca, Altahuallpa was kidnapped; and after the delivery of Incan gold to the Spaniards, he was killed by them (Wachtel 1977, pp. 21–23).

In terms of ideology and the ideological role in the reproduction of the Incan social formation, it should be pointed out that both Hernán Cortés and Francisco Pizarro were at least partially able to overturn the indigenous orders because their presence corresponded to indigenous religious ideas regarding the return of the gods; or, as in the case of Pizarro, the belief that the band of mysterious bearded soldiers had been sent by the gods to avenge the "legitimate" claim of Huascar—the true son of the god—against the usurper, Altahuallpa. To put this in structural terms, the Spaniards—through sheer coincidence—were able to intrude into the structure of the Incan mode of production by inserting (or having inserted) the meaning of their presence directly, at least momentarily, into the ideological element of the indigenous social reproduction process.

This initial ideological intrusion was quickly followed with the establishment of Spanish state administration, repressive apparatus, and a formal ideological apparatus through the Roman Catholic Church. At the political level, the Spanish were able to insert themselves into the equivalent place of the Incan nobility. At the ideological level, the Catholic priests set about the task of replacing the format, if not the meaning, of indigenous religious celebrations and rituals with European Christian formats.

This led to what Wachtel refers to (in the French equivalent) as "destructuration" of the Incan state. The Incan nobility was displaced by the Spanish, and the kind of reciprocity between *kuraka* and ruler changed, the *kurakas* maintained the role of intermediary class:

> The Spanish system could only function with the collaboration of the local chiefs, who continued to play the role of the intermediaries in the levying of tribute . . . *kuraka* collaboration was usually obtained [by the Spanish], either spontaneously or by force. By their cooperation they retained, to a certain extent, a privileged status (Wachtel 1977, p. 123).

SPANISH ADMINISTRATION

If only because of the distances involved, the Spanish monarchy was not able to assert direct control over its American possessions. The bureaucracy that Spain constructed to administer its South American possession often took years to pass along executive orders and responses:

> Far from the centers of power, in the hinterlands of the empire, powerful governors followed the unspoken norm of "obeying without executing" any royal ordinances that hurt their own interests (Larson and Wasserstrom 1983, p. 50).

Brooke Larson argues that this lack of formal control by the Spanish monarch allowed the local Spanish governors to extract excess tribute from indigenous communities through the use of "forced commodity consumption" or "*repartimientos de mercancias.*" In order to extract surplus value from the indigenous communities, governors organized "coercive trading activities on an unprecedented scale. They forced the hapless inhabitants of Indian villages to accept consignments of alcohol, textiles, plough shares, foodcrops, trinkets and other commodities procured from wholesale merchants in distant cities or ports" (1983, p. 51).

This forced consumption was made possible through the use of indigenous local leaders: "The key links in this [distribution network] were usually native authorities or *mestizo* underlings who forced peasant households to acquire allotments of goods for a fixed sum of money or a stipulated cash crop" (Larson and Wasserstrom 1983, p. 51). Significantly, this scheme of extraction involved the *kuraka* ("native authority") in the role of intermediary between the ruling class and the direct producer. It should be stressed that this relationship of exploiter to exploited (or ruling class to direct producer) was not a relationship of production that can be characterized as capitalist. The intermediary class in this situation was playing a double role of mediating political domination of the indigenous population (discussed below) and of mediating economic extraction from one mode of production to another. Even the forced production of a cash crop for the purpose of trading or realizing cash did not force the *indígena* from his or her own relations of production.[12] According to Larson, even in the Cochabamba Valley where the *repartimientos de mercancias* had perhaps their greatest impact: "Social differentiation within the Cochabamba peasantry would have to advance much further before social pressures and uncertainties would turn a sector of the peasantry into a migrant work force in the distant industrial mines" (Larson 1988, p. 8).

In general, indigenous leaders who resisted Spanish domination were removed from their leadership positions (even if in technical violation of royal law), and indigenous leaders (or those who made claim to leadership positions) who gave their loyalty (or cooperation) to the particular Spanish governor under threat of imprisonment and/or from economic incentive were advanced on the basis of Spanish-derived authority. An important implication of this new role for the *kurakas* as intermediary to a different mode of production was the increased stress on the ideological support to the political element.[13] That is, with two modes facing each other—each with its own ideology—how could the political authority of the "supervisor" be supported by the ideological element of either mode? The answer (demonstrated over time) was that there could not be any sustained ideological support from either mode for the political authority of the *kuraka* in his colonial role. We would expect, then, that relations of domination would have to rely upon violence and personal corruption. And, in fact, this was the case.

As Wachtel points out, the accepted notion among historians, that after the conquest the *kurakas* exercised tyrannical powers, may in some ways be partially correct. The *kurakas* themselves had to rely more upon violence than ideology to maintain their authority, which, in turn, was exercised on behalf of the Spanish. In this way, to the casual observer, the increased use of violence by the colonial *kurakas* would make them appear more tyrannical than the *kurakas* of the Incan social formation. Nonetheless, this need to resort to violent repression was one symptom of a loss of political authority. The *kurakas* who collaborated with the Spanish against the indigenous people were destroying their own "prestige." They were therefore forced to assert their authority despotically:

> Eventually cause and effect coalesced: decline in the power of the *kurakas* led to a fall in the amount of tribute they received and their impoverishment compelled them, if they wished to maintain their prestige, to look for profits at the expense of the members of the community: but by so doing, they accelerated the destruction of this same prestige (1977, pp. 130–31).

Yet the indigenous population within the *ayllu* refused to leave or disregard the social relations of their community:

> Garci Diez constantly insists that they worked "against their will:" if the Spanish merchants offered money directly to the Indians, they would refuse it. They did the work only because the *kurakas* ordered them to do so. And in turn the latter resorted to force to be obeyed (Wachtel 1977, p. 130).

Although the Spanish were able to entice and force cooperation from *kurakas,* Larson makes the point that despite the efforts of the Spanish state to turn the Andean chiefs into dependents of the state in the late sixteenth century, it failed to establish a separate hierarchy of authority that responded directly to its demands. The *kuraka* never became a part of the official Spanish administrative apparatus: "In the eighteenth century the native Andean elite in many regions was a tightly knit group which still exercised many of the rights, responsibilities and claims that their ancestors had enjoyed" (Larson and Wasserstrom 1983, p. 60). The class place of the *kuraka* as intermediary retained its function as a bridge between separate modes of production with radically different social relations and corresponding ideologies. Because of these radical distinctions, no effective *kuraka* could be simply an administrative agent in a Spanish bureaucracy. As noted above, if a *kuraka* were one-sided Spanish (or solely depended upon his authority from the Spanish), he would lose real authority (political legitimacy) with the *ayllu.*

This contradiction over the question of political authority meant that while the articulation of the two modes of production required and thus reinforced the role of the *kuraka* as intermediary, it would also mean that the "loyalty" of the *kuraka* would always be problematic from the standpoint of the Spanish. If we can assume that the effect of the ideological forces acting upon the *kuraka* were as strong as the profit-motive forces (referred to by Wachtel),[14] then, just as there would have to be the continual use of violence by the Spanish—if only to assure the authority of those *kurakas* installed by them— there would be *kurakas* who remained loyal to their *ayllus*. The definition of "loyalty" involves acting at the behest of ideology wherein the subject acts according to his or her perception of what is "right"; rather than acting on the basis of "personal gain" (i.e., "corruption"). To take this somewhat deeper, one of the factors here is what may be viewed as a competition between ideologies for the capture of the mediating class. That is, within the reproduction process of the relationship between two modes of opposing ideologies, which ideology will dominate or determine the place of the intermediary? For the *kuraka* to retain legitimacy within the indigenous community he must be granted his supervisorial authority through indigenous ideology.

Conceivably an Adam Smithian liberal *kuraka* might have existed who honestly believed that selling his services (management skill) to the highest bidder was the correct thing to do. But, even in such a scenario, if this particular *kuraka* were perceived by his community as simply selling his service to the highest bidder, he would lose his authority (and consequently also lose the quality that made him useful to the Spanish/capitalist side of the social formation). As discussed in Chapters 3 and 5, co-opted *campesinado* leaders did lose their authority because of this contradiction. Larson comments that because "some *kurakas* in these decades were heroic in their resistance and challenge to colonial authorities in their own provinces while other lords were corrupt, opportunistic collaborators attests to the historically ambiguous and contradictory roles they played on the interface of two worlds" (1983, p. 60).[15] In such a situation we could expect the constant threat of rebellion from the indigenous population led by the "loyal" *kurakas*.

RESISTANCE AND REBELLION

The execution of Túpac Amaru at the hands of the Spanish in 1572 ended the official Incan resistance to Spanish colonization of the Andes. Amaru's death did not end the indigenous population's ideology of resistance. In conjunction with one early attempt at indigenous insurrection against Spanish rule, a religious doctrine known as *Taqui Ongo* was spread through the provinces of central Peru in the 1560s. From this center, the movement seems to have extended as far as Lima in the west, Cuzco in the east, and to La Paz in the south (Wachtel 1977, p. 179). Preachers of this "sect":

travelled from village to village exhorting the Indians to restore the cult of *huacas* [gods] destroyed by the Christians. They revived these gods in ritual "resurrection" ceremonies, pouring libations of *chicha* and making offerings of maize at the ruins of the holy places. . . . Joining *Taqui Ongo* was like crossing a divide: it confirmed the rift between the Spanish and Indian worlds (1977, p. 182).

According to the doctrine of this religion, Spanish rule would soon end. Indigenous gods were stronger than the Christian God and the *huacas* were preparing a new battle against the Christian God, the result of which would be the banishment of the Spanish from the country. In a result similar to that of the *katarista* movement within Bolivia in the 1980s, this early "indigenous movement" brought the "two cultures, Spanish and Indian, face to face, in order to exalt the latter" (1977, p. 180). Once discovered by the Spanish priesthood, this subversive ideology was ruthlessly suppressed. As well, the followers and priests of this religion were probably discouraged by the death of Amaru. By the 1570s all trace of *Taqui Ongo* had vanished (1977, p. 183).

Through the 1600s and 1700s the indigenous population developed the idea that the king of Spain (and his legal system) would protect them. That is, indigenous ideology incorporated the idea that the king of Spain was a benevolent seeker of justice.[16] From the 1740s through the 1770s the indigenous population left their communities for months or even years to testify in the Colonial High Court in Chuquisaca:

> Patiently they submitted their petitions for royal redress and retribution. Through the endless litigation, Andean chiefs (kurakas) and other members of village hierarchies played a vital role in mobilizing peasants and articulating grievances before the colonial magistrates (Larson and Wasserstrom 1983, p. 59).

These legal efforts to end the forced consumption of the *repartimientos de mercancias* and other abuses of the *corregidores* had little effect on Spanish policy. Not until the rebellion of Túpac Amaru II in 1780 did the Spanish implement new tribute procedures:

> It was only [in November, 1780], in a moment of terror, that the Peruvian viceroy suppressed the *repartimientos* on the grounds of "the injuries and wrongs which they cause the Indians whose complaints have flooded the tribunals." But the measure came too late to prevent a wave of violence from engulfing the land (Larson and Wasserstrom 1983, p. 61).

This rebellion from 1780 to 1782, though the largest, was by no means the only rebellion of the 1700s. Steve Stern states that "well over a hundred times during the years 1720–1790, the native Andean peoples of Peru and Bolivia, sometimes accompanied or led by dissident *castas* (mixed racial groups) and whites, rose up in violent defiance of colonial authorities" (1987, p. 34). Besides Túpac Amaru II (previously a *kuraka,* José Gabriel Condorcanqui), the other leaders of the revolt were Tomás Katari and Julián Apasa (who took the name Túpac Katari):[17]

> [From Cuzco to northern Argentina] native insurgents who joined the rebel leader, Túpac Amaru, or who expressed their solidarity, rose up and massacred *corregidores.* Túpac Amaru himself declared that he sought retribution on behalf of his people "for the wrongs inflicted on them by various persons, such as the *corregidores* and Europeans." During the early phases of the struggle, his proclaimed goal was neither nationalist nor millenarian, but simply that "this class of official [the *corregidores*] be completely removed and their *repartimientos* ended . . ." (Larson and Wasserstrom 1983, p. 61).

The crown agreed to these demands and issued orders, in May 1781, to abolish all *repartimientos* in Peru. One year later the *corregidores* were replaced by professional, salaried bureaucrats from Spain.

As discussed by Leon Campbell (1987) and Larson (1983), the rebellion, though widespread, was internally divided by rivalries among particular *kurakas* and differing goals. In fact, Larson goes so far as to argue that these moments of rebellion and violent countermoves to Spanish oppression helped to increase "the internal economic and ethnic divisions in Andean rural society which had deepened over the course of the eighteenth century" (1983, p. 62).

THE REPUBLIC

One major problem for the new government was the decline in revenue from silver mining. Revenue from mining had already peaked in the early decades of the 1600s and the war had further disastrous effects on the local miners. Potosí's 40 silver refining mills in 1803 had decreased to 15 by 1825. This stagnation of the private sector was also reflected in the public economy. Whereas the prime sources of government income under the crown had been mining, production, and sales tax, the republican government relied mostly upon a head tax on indigenous landowners. Thus in the budget of 1846, the head tax on the indigenous population was the largest single source of government revenue and accounted for 43 percent of government income. If the tax on coca production, which was a product consumed only the the indigenous population, is added, then direct taxation of the indigenous population accounted for 50 percent of all government revenues (Klein 1969, pp. 4–5).

Herbert Klein describes the indigenous population as a separate society of rural subsistence farmers whose only contact with the other society was in the economic sphere:

> These two societies were hierarchically arranged; and the non-Indian minority, the only part of the nation truly aware of national existence, totally exploited the Indian majority, both through the discriminatory taxing system, and even more importantly in its control over the land (1969, p. 7).

In the early 1800s the land was divided between an expanding *latifundia* system controlled by the oligarchy and the *ayllus* (or "village communities") of the Aymarans and Quechuans. The indigenous communities comprised several categories of land-owning and landless families (*originarios, agregados,* and *forasteros sin tierra*), and in 1846 they accounted for an estimated 621,468 persons. The white hacendados and their families were another 23,107 persons, while the landless *indígenas* on the haciendas (*colonos* or *pongos*) numbered some 360,000 persons.

Klein comments that the state that emerged after the wars and declaration of independence of August 6, 1825, was not essentially different from the previous state (1969, p. 1). However, the Bolivian "oligarchy" that was previously hindered by the Spanish monarchy's "protection" of the indigenous communities created a state that reflected their interests alone. Unhindered by the monarchy or not, the new state was confronted with the problem of how to control the indigenous communities and make use of the surplus value that could be generated within the communities. The Bolivian Republic attempted to solve the problem, first, by attempting to make use of a head tax on the indigenous communities extracted through the *kurakas* and *recaudadores*. Second, it attempted to solve the problem by usurping indigenous land promoting the extension of the hacienda system (as a mechanism of labor extraction) into the areas of the communities and, perhaps more importantly, through the capture of labor from the indigenous communities.

EFFECTS ON THE INDIGENOUS COMMUNITIES (*AYLLUS*)

The de facto division of the Bolivian social formation into two worlds was, after some hesitation, essentially recognized *de jure* by the new state. From the point of view of the capitalist side of the social formation this division was necessary for the capitalist side to maintain political and economic domination of the indigenous side. If only because of the difference in numbers, the *indígena* could not be allowed to be a citizen with the protection of the state equal to that of the *criollos* (or of the *"cholos"*—*indígenas* who made the "change of clothes" and entered the capitalist side). This social division was also enforced by the indigenous population itself. Writers such as Herbert Klein (1969) and Andrew Pearse (1972) emphasize the fact that the *kurakas* defended this division in the interest of protecting their own privileges. However, it is also clearly the case that the ideology within the indigenous communities was not compatible with the liberal notions of individualism, of which there was at least initially an attempt to apply to the indigenous population as a justification for the payment of individual taxes to the government. By 1829 new decrees were promulgated, which once again recognized the ethnic status of *indígena*. These decrees assigned limited servile labor obligations to the *indígena* toward the persons of the parish priests and certain "local administrative officials"[18] (Pearse 1972, p. 263).

The initial attempt of the application of the liberal principle of the individual ownership of property (if only for the purposes of taxation) ran up against opposition from the ruling class because of the logically ensuing implication of the rights of citizenship. It aroused opposition from the indigenous communities because it was contrary to the notion of collective ownership. Through a process of protest and accommodation the indigenous communities were able to gain some reprieve from monetary payments of taxes and were able to substitute a tribute system of labor and goods. Nonetheless, cash payments were derived from the indigenous population through the sales of lowland grains and flour. Only in moments of extreme dearth would livestock (a form of savings for the *indígena*) be converted to cash. Highland produce, such as fresh or desiccated potato, was sold in the local mining centers when demand was sufficient, but most of these highland crops went to subsistence (Platt 1987, p. 290).

The individuals who acted as intermediaries in this process were usually "cholos" who occupied the position of *corregidor* (governor of a province) and *recaudadores* who acted as intermediaries between the governor and their particular community. These *recaudadores* enjoyed a series of privileges: each ethnic group offered its *recaudador* personal (household) services on a rotating basis. The given community also provided collective labor in the common lands, sowing, tending, and harvesting the crops of the recaudador. Those *indígenas* who wished could offer instead a measure of potatoes, wheat, and oats. Each *indígena* also had to provide a chicken for the collectors at each semestral ceremony, and each local community chief (*jilaqata*) serving under the collector had to pay him a peso at each ceremony. Each *recaudador* could consider himself a sort of mini-hacendado, although his land was in fact the common land, originally designed to serve the interests of the collective (Platt 1987, p. 291).

Between 1831 and 1839, the tribute system described above coexisted with legislation that kept a "discreet silence" over the processes of tribute payment to the *recaudador*. Nonetheless, the *ayllu* commons continued to decline. Although various administrations pursued separate policies regarding land and tribute collection, the republican government never relinquished the legal theory that land was to be individually owned. The ideological basis was thus set by the time President Mariano Melgarejo began selling community lands to individuals.

In 1866 Melgarejo declared all community lands to be state property and fixed a sum of money at which the *indígenas* could purchase the land they occupied. After the passage of a certain number of months the land would be considered public property and for sale to anyone. The result of this decree (and corollary decrees) was the sale of 356 communities to outsiders by 1869 (Rivera 1979 [*Allpanchis*], p. 198). Much of this land sale resulted in resistance from the *indígenas* and many of the new landowners were unable to make real their new claim to the property of the *comunidades*. Upon the fall of Melgarejo in 1870 the new government declared all acts of the Melgarejo government null. At the same time, the new government declared that it would study conditions for authorizing the right of property to the *indígenas*.

The law of "*exvinculación*" of October 5, 1874, initiated a new phase in the extension of the latifundia. Individual families who once dealt with the state through the intermediaries of their own leadership were exposed directly to a "new petty bourgeoisie" from the capitalist mode of production of auditors, lawyers, and judges. This action had the effect of replacing, or at least shunting aside, the indigenous-based class of intermediaries. It also meant that people who had no experience in dealing with the state apparatus of the capitalist side were suddenly exposed to the manipulations of that "other society." Through intimidation and fraud, former *comunidad* land was transferred into the hands of the hacendados. Between the years 1881 and 1899, sales continued to increase, and after a short respite in the late 1890s (due to the rebellions of the Federalistas and of Pablo Zárte Willka) transfers of community land to hacendados continued until 1920 (Rivera 1979, pp. 201-2).

HACIENDA AS POINT OF ECONOMIC ARTICULATION AND POLITICAL CONTROL

The segment of the indigenous population that found its occupation on the hacienda was known as the *yanaconas*. These individuals were those who for various reasons did not belong to a particular *ayllu*. An original source of hacienda laborers, *yanaconas* were those individuals who served as slaves to the Inca; as such, they had been separated from their original community. During the period of the Republic more individuals became *yanaconas* as they sought refuge from the *mit'a*; also, as the land of the communities were usurped by the *criollos*, many *indígenas* had no choice[19] but to relocate on a hacienda. By 1952 perhaps two thirds of the peasantry lived and worked on haciendas. Relations of production on the hacienda were much like those on the estates of feudal Europe. The full tenant was known as the "first person" and owed four days of labor per week on the fields of hacendado, using his own oxen and plough. In return, he received the use of a full field for cultivation as well as a lot of land for his house and garden. The "second person" was obligated to provide three days of labor per week. Sons living with service tenants had to give one day of work per week in nonagricultural tasks, such as making adobe bricks, cutting firewood, and so forth. It was common for a third category of family to live on the hacienda with right to a house and garden lot only, and owing two days of labor per week to the hacienda (Pearse 1972, p. 266).

Although there are many accounts of the use of violence to enforce labor discipline on the *colonos*, these relations of production fit within the pattern of mutual reciprocity that characterized the relations of production in the indigenous communities. Referring to the colonial court records of a case in the 1780s, Larson reports complaints brought by the tenants (in this case "*arrenderos*" who were tenants who theoretically had some leeway to negotiate the conditions of exchange for their labor) who argued that the new owner of their hacienda in the Cochabamba Valley was unfair: "Almarás [the new owner] failed to honor the implicit code of reciprocity. He demanded more labor and gave less in return than had been the case in the past, and in the process he jeopardized his own legitimacy and status" (Larson 1988, p. 201).

The advent of regular peasant markets in the central valleys signaled the emergence of a channel outside the channels controlled by landlords and large merchants, through which peasants could trade among themselves on their own terms and in accord with their own marketplace etiquette" (Larson 1988, p. 203).

This market activity independent of the hacendados in the Cochabamba area meant that much of the surplus generated by the *campesinado*, who were participants in the hacienda system, remained within the economy of the indigenous population (i.e., not subject to direct transfer to the capitalist side). It also marked what became a long-term area of competition between the landlord and the tenant.

Andrew Pearse recounted an interview in which the informant described the day of the opening of railway traffic between Cochabamba and the mining centers in 1914. The hacendados arrived at the station only to find that the *campesinos—colonos* and free—were already there, selling quantities of produce to the buyers who had arrived from Oruro and the mining encampments. Many of the hacendados who had borrowed heavily in anticipation of improved commercial conditions found themselves with financial problems because of the peasant competition and were forced to parcel out and sell their haciendas. Pearse goes on to argue that this ability of the *campesinado* in the Cochabamba area to compete commercially with the hacendados was in direct contradiction to the enforcement of servile duties, and was at least one reason why the *campesinos* in the Cochabamba area led the *campesinado* agitation for land reform in 1953 (Pearse 1972, p. 404).

Probably the most important general point that can be drawn from the above discussion is that the *indígena* of the hacienda did not stop being *indígena*. Although it is true that the hacienda was able, in effect, to capture indigenous labor in a form of what might be called tight articulation, the *indígena* retained noncapitalist social relations of production. That is, in the instance of the hacienda where the economic form of articulation involved labor immobilization (as opposed to migration), that immobilization (unlike the situation of, for example, the capture of former peasants within the urban factory) did not mean (or lead to) the dissolution of indigenous economic (or ideological) processes. The articulation of the hacienda remained articulation between two different modes of production precisely because indigenous labor relations were not transformed.

In his essay, "Results of the Immediate Process of Production," Marx made the distinction between "formal subsumption"—where relations of production remain noncapitalist—and "real subsumption"—where relations of production are capitalist—of the peasantry. The hacienda system may be seen as a case of tight articulation in which, perhaps unexpectedly, the subsumption of the peasantry is formal rather than real. In Chapter 5, I argue that the effect of the 1953 agrarian reform was to change this tight articulation to a loose articulation. Because the "real subsumption" of indigenous labor did not occur at the site of the hacienda, it was unrealistic for Bolivian state planners to expect the *campesinado* to become capitalist simply because their labor power was freed from the bonds of the hacienda.

INDIGENOUS REBELLIONS

According to Silvia Rivera Cusicanqui, the property transfers initiated by Mariano Melgarejo were accompanied by the beginning of a condition of permanent indigenous rebellion that exploded into the large scale rebellions of 1895 to 1896. In August 1896 the rebellion reached its apogee in an uprising that extended nearly the entire length of the altiplano between La Paz and Oruro. These rebellions were brutally repressed by the military. Working initially in alliance with the Liberals in 1899, the indigenous forces of Pablo Zárate Willka engaged in a massive indigenous rebellion. Zárate and a group of *kurakas* mobilized the "indiada" of provinces of Sicasica, Muñecas, Pacajes, Ingavi, Omasuyos e Inquisivi de La Paz, and some provinces of the Departments of Potosi and Cochabamba in the "greatest indigenous rebellion in the history" of the Republic. However, once the Liberals had accomplished their objectives they turned against their indigenous allies who had pursued the separate objectives of reconquering the land and "exterminating the white exploiters." The indigenous rebellion was suppressed and the leadership was executed. The indigenous movement was virtually paralyzed and the expansion of the latifundia system proceeded (Rivera 1979, pp. 203-4).[20] With a generation of leadership dead, the indigenous movement would not be resurrected again until the 1930s and 1940s with the organization of the *campesinado* movement.

CONCLUSION

The willingness of the *kurakas* to bring their case against the oppression of the *corregidores* to the Spanish courts indicates that the "practices" of the Spanish ideological apparatuses did meet with at least some success. Even the indigenous rebel chiefs of 1780 to 1782 based their claim to the legitimacy of their use of violence against the local Spanish and *criollo* population on the claim that the king of Spain, with his sense of justice, would order the rebel chiefs into action. Nonetheless, the fact that the *kuraka* did remain within an intermediary class place, and that the hacienda acted as a mechanism of control without the breakup of indigenous relations of production, was itself a result of the fact that the indigenous population as a whole retained their own mode of production complete with mechanisms for reproduction of their own ideology. The indigenous population as a whole rarely entered into capitalist relations of production, and in no case did it merge into the mode of production brought by the Spanish.

With the death of the leadership of the Zárate Willka Rebellion the *indígenista* movement in Bolivia was effectively suppressed until the growth of a new generation of leaders and the impact of the Chaco War on the "rank and file" of the *campesinado*. Meanwhile, on the capitalist side of the Bolivian social formation, the late 1800s and early 1900s saw the re-emergence of an export-dominated economy and the emergence of a university-educated class of new petty bourgeoisie. This new class, in conjunction with the radicalized miners and reconstituted peasantry, frustrated with the inefficiencies of the old oligarchy—made apparent in both the War of the Pacific in the 1870s and the Chaco War in the 1930s—would seek to enlarge the "nation" in the revolution of 1952. These class developments and political consequences are taken up in the next chapter.

NOTES

1. A tributary mode of production is a mode that is characterized by merchant activity and the extraction of value from direct producers largely by extra-economic force. See Wolff (1982, pp. 79–80) for a discussion of this mode. The concern in this chapter (as throughout) is not with this tributary/capitalist mode of production; rather the primary concern is with explaining the articulation between the two modes from the standpoint of the indigenous side. However, it is accepted that the mode of production in which the Spanish were involved when they penetrated South America was a tributary mode and its expansion entailed a process of "primitive, precapitalist" capital accumulation. This does not mean that Spain was on a linear trajectory to the development of capitalism. To the contrary, its *pre*capitalist activities may well have been what deterred development of capitalist relations of production in Spain. But the "treasure" (as opposed to "wealth") that was removed from the Spanish colonies was, perhaps, part of the development of capitalism in northern Europe. The aim of this study, however, is to avoid this subject of analysis for the sake of concentrating on social and political relations within Bolivia. The origin of this aim lies in the very consideration of the key processes of modes of production (and thus the subject of its analysis) within relations of production rather than relations of exchange.

2. Although it is true that in the situations examined by Poulantzas, he uses this idea

("forms of production") to explain "class fractions"—e.g., comprador bourgeoisie and national bourgeoisie—as opposed to separate class place categories, the Bolivian situation warrants the conceptualization of a separate class place at the ideological and political point of articulation.

3. In his 1982 article, Deiterich implies that the internal organization of the *ayllu* moved to a class structure. I do not believe that the evidence demonstrated in his own article or the general literature support that conclusion.

4. See Joseph Bastien's *Mountain of the Condor* (1978) for a description of a twentieth-century *ayllu* in Bolivia.

5. By no means does this imply that the lack of an iron plow, for example, causes preponderantly agrarian societies. Whereas it is true that social formations that require nonagrarian labor need a level of technology that increases agrarian labor productivity, I do not accept the notion that the "forces of production" are an ultimate or sufficient motive force of history. Agrarian, noncapitalist social formations do not necessarily come apart when someone introduces the plough and horse.

6. Murra (1986) begins his article on the expansion of the Inca state with the doubts expressed by the Swedish historian Ake Wedin. Wedin argued that there was no occidental precedent for such rapid expansion and challenged the veracity of oral dynastic tradition.

7. This kind of arrangement continues to exist and is described in Joseph Bastien's ethnographic research of an Andean *ayllu* in his book *Mountain of the Condor*.

8. Many sources, including Murra, use the word "lord" for this position. I suspect that usage of such words stems from the Spanish description of the local leadership who, in Spanish eyes, would be most similar to the landed aristocrat.

9. To clarify, the word "Inca" literally refers, as it does here, to the monarch or ruler himself.

10. Children of the women of the harem, or nonprincipal wives, of the Inca did not have hereditary rights.

11. As discussed in Chapter 2, it should be emphasized that the "knowledge" of the reproduction of the social formation is an "ideological" knowledge. By this I mean that the knowledge of various reproduction techniques is knowledge of techniques that have validity because people (including the people who are dominated through the use of those techniques) believe that the techniques have validity. For example, in a capitalist social formation, the "maximization of efficiency" is seen by nearly all as a "good," "valid" principle. The people who learn the techniques for "maximizing efficiency" are hired by firms to be "managers." The "fact" that the "maximization of efficiency" is for the benefit of maximizing return on investment for the stockholders—and that it will invariably result in such things as the lowest possible wages for workers, a tendency toward unsafe work conditions, damages to the environment (and thus the health) of the population—is seen, if at all, as a "unfortunate, but unavoidable," secondary problem. Neither workers nor society as a whole often challenge the validity of the authority of the supervisor or of the ideology that both supports that authority and is the "knowledge" of, for example, the professor of "business management."

12. There are important implications here involving the effect of this coerced consumption on the social relations of the *ayllu* populations in the Andean Valleys (where the Spanish were most able to have access to the native population). Larson follows out some of these implications in her book, *Colonialism and Agrarian Transformation in*

Bolivia (1988). Chapter 5 makes use of this colonial experience to help explain the greater commercial "spirit" of the indigenous population of the Cochabamba area compared to the population of the Altiplano. In fact, as noted by Larson and discussed in Murra (1986), this difference in behavior can be traced to the rule of the Incas who had driven the original population from the Cochabamba Valley and had turned it into a relatively large-scale, specialized agricultural zone—repopulated by the Incas with a population specializing in this high output agriculture.

13. This point on ideology anticipates the discussion taken up in Chapter 6 regarding the ethnicity (or racism) of the *indígenista* argument. One might well argue that the reliance upon ideological mechanisms of social reproduction would be no greater in the Colonial formation than in the Incan social formation. That is, in both cases the dominant class was of a foreign entity that had conquered and claimed political authority over an ethnically separate community. And, as noted in the discussion above, the Inca relied upon violence often to maintain control of rebellious *ayllus*. Two responses to such an argument can be made. First, the ideological practices of the Incan social formation were in accord or could easily conform with the practices of the conquered *ayllus*. This, in turn, was related to a method of surplus extraction that was compatible with the reciprocal relations of production found in the mode of production of the *ayllus*. Second, as noted in Chapter 6 the political position of current groups—such as the CSUTCB— who claim an *indígenista* foundation are not arguing for some literal return to *ayllu* divisions and/or a return to an Incan-like structure of domination. Nevertheless, as I understand the position, the CSUTCB makes its claim to an indigenous ideological foundation because it would base the development of Bolivia on an ideology compatible with the relations of production of the *ayllu*.

14. It is tempting, but I think absurd, to put this notion into market terminology. How much was the cooperation of a *kuraka* worth? For how much would a *kuraka* sell his "organic" loyalty to his *ayllu*?

15. Eric R. Wolf asserts in his 1982 work that the *kurakas* who defended the integrity of the communities from Spanish abuses were merely pursuing their own self-interest. That is, Wolf argues that the *kurakas*, put in place by the Spanish, simply acted to protect their own power. Wolf oversimplifies this aspect of the problematic by attributing the liberal notion of the pursuit of individual self-interest to everyone. As discussed in the text, *kurakas* who were resistant to the demands of the *corregidores* were replaced by rivals who had the support of the Spanish. These *kurakas* were apparently acting from self-interest as the Spanish sought to grant political legitimacy to these *kurakas* by Spanish approval of authority. However, the source of authority and direction of loyalty (and ideological matter) even in the case of these *kurakas*, much less than those who did not rely upon the Spanish to assert authority, cannot be satisfactorily explained in terms of pursuit of self-interest. I agree with Larson that many *kurakas* acted "heroically" in the sense that they were loyal to their communities and acted according to that loyalty to defend their communities.

16. Indeed, having universalized the notion of a just king for all, the indigenous population—even at the height of rebellion—posed the king of Spain as a weapon against the local Spanish and Creoles, arguing that the king would permit the use of force against the injustice of the local Spanish.

17. According to Leon Campbell (in Stern 1987, p. 132), Túpac Katari represented a racist ideology in contrast to the political opposition of the Amaruistas to Spanish rule.

Indigenous Social Formation 57

At one point near the end of the rebellion, while encamped outside the besieged city of La Paz, Túpac Katari ordered the execution of anyone who could not prove he or she was Aymaran. (Amaru means serpent in Quechua, Katari means serpent in Aymara).

18. I assume that Pearse is referring to the *recaudadores* described in the text below.

19. A point to be noted here is that this enclosurelike process did not generally lead to a "proletarianization" of the peasantry. Urban capitalism was too weak to make a demand for labor power, and the new hacienda owners were in need of laborers.

20. For an extensive history of the Zárate rebellion, see Ramiro Condarco Morales, *Zárate, el "Temible" Willka; historia de la rebelion indígena de 1899*, 2nd ed. (La Paz: published by author, 1982).

Chapter 4
Review of Postrevolutionary Bolivian Politics

This chapter describes the configuration of the class alliance among the national bourgeoisie, new petty bourgeoisie,[1] the miners, and the peasantry. It was this combination of corresponding class-based political forces that led to the revolutionary conjuncture of 1952. This chapter also traces the political development of the peasantry from the Chaco War of the 1930s to the mid-1980s, and includes a discussion of the politics of Bolivian political leaders and the policies of the state regarding the *campesinado* following the agrarian reform. A central argument is that the Bolivian state did not promote rural development because such a policy was viewed by state decisionmakers in the 1950s and 1960s as neither essential to the Bolivian economy, nor politically expedient.

The special partnership that all Bolivian regimes of that period sought to maintain with the *campesinado* was a necessary arrangement for the state as it directed its attentions to the politics of continuous confrontation with the miners. Political failure of the Bolivian state, beginning in the early 1970s, to maintain the support of the *campesinado* was mainly the result of an ideological unity among the *campesinado* that was used to drive a new (or renewed) political movement, *katarismo*. Also during this period, the political economy of Bolivia was shifting. With the issue made explicitly sharp by the sudden drop of the price of tin in late 1985, state policymakers were coming to the view that development of capitalist farming in the *indígena* regions of Bolivia was essential to the health, if not the survival, of the capitalist economy as a whole in Bolivia. *Katarismo* and the changed policy goals of the Bolivian state made for new loci of conflict on the political landscape that were indicative of the subterranean historical forces of movement and fracture.

The three major "social blocs" that determined the revolutionary conjuncture in 1952 were the national bourgeoisie in alliance with the new petty bourgeoisie (composed of bureaucrats, managers, professionals, and intellectuals), the miners, and the peasantry. This coalition, represented politically by the

Movimiento Nacionalista Revolucionario (MNR) and led by Victor Paz Estenssoro and Hernán Siles Zuazo, would fragment soon enough. The conjuncture (i.e., the political crisis in which these three blocs struggled together against the traditional ruling class [mine owners and hacendados] and which culminated in the 1952 revolution) is elucidated in terms of the political groups and alliances that affected the revolution and were part of its fallout.

We turn first to a short prerevolution history of the three groups and then to the postrevolution alliances—most importantly that of the *campesinado* and the state against the miners.

SOCIAL BLOCS AND POLITICAL DEVELOPMENTS

National and New Petty Bourgeoisie

"New petty bourgeoisie" designates a group separate from that group labeled petty bourgeoisie (i.e., shopkeepers and artisans) or "traditional petty bourgeoisie." It is also a "new" group in that it was a new class in the 1930s (i.e., at the time of the Chaco War) evolving from that group of individuals who were relatively well educated and took employment in the state bureaucracy, the banking industry, mining management, education, law, medicine, and the military officer corps. This group emerged in the conditions of an export-led economy in which the state, whether occupied by conservatives or liberals, had set for itself the task of building economic infrastructure (Klein 1969, pp. 16-17). Although much of this new class was directly employed by the state, its source of income was ultimately dependent upon the income of the silver and tin mines.[2] This was not a new petty bourgeoisie that was developing in conjunction with a significantly expanding industrial sector. There was, however, a growing, if weak, national economy that fueled the development of a number of capitalist enterprises not directly dependent upon major export. The presence of this class place can be inferred from the information that in 1950, 14 percent of the Bolivian gross domestic product was in the secondary sector of manufacturing and construction (in Doria Medina 1986, p. 37).[3] As this bloc developed, it simultaneously developed a nationalist ideology that excluded what was perceived as the corrupt and even treasonous[4] oligarchical interests of the *rosca*.[5]

The roots of this nationalism were seen by most Bolivianists as planted in the Chaco War. Although it was by no means an ultimate cause of this nationalism, the Chaco War was both a stimulus to and a symptom of this new nationalism. Further, this war had serious consequences as a stimulus of change in self-perception for the thousands of *campesinos* who were brought together as soldiers on the battlefields and as prisoners in the Paraguayan internment camps.

Responding to the calls of patriotism, many idealistic sons of the new petty bourgeoisie served as lower echelon officers in that war and discovered that the Bolivian "nation" at least contained, if not included, a population and culture previously excluded from the accepted concept of "Bolivian nation." At the same time, the war dragged thousands of "Bolivian" *indios* or "*campesinos*" (many at gunpoint) into a conflict for a cause of which they knew nothing. For the first time the *campesinos* were shoulder to shoulder with people of similar life situations, people who were, they discovered, their "countrymen."

The war was declared against Paraguay in July of 1932 by Bolivian President Daniel Salamanca ostensibly over a territorial dispute in the Chaco. Salamanca, who had come to power via a military coup in 1930 and represented the interests of the traditional ruling class, used preparation for the war to justify repression of domestic political opposition. The war itself was regarded by observers in 1932 as an easy victory for the German-trained army of Bolivia. Instead, the war ended in humiliating defeat for Bolivia in June 1936. According to James Malloy, "the Paraguayans out-thought, out-fought, and simply out-lasted the bewildered Bolivians most of whom were fighting in an environment so foreign as to be another world" (1971, p. 73).

Malloy asserts that the Chaco War was Bolivia's first "national" war—indeed its first real "national" effort of any kind. "The Chaco War was converted into a nationalist crusade. To drive the mobilization and sublimate the sacrifices occasioned by the war, jingoism and patriotic fervor became the order of the day" (1971, p. 73). At the same time, with the notion of loyalty to the "nation" as opposed to the leaders, lower ranking officers experienced firsthand the effects of the incompetence and corruption of higher echelon officers and political leaders. As Robert Alexander notes, these lower ranking officers were drawn largely from the "middle and upper middle classes" and "suffered alongside their troops the privations of the campaigns. . . . Many of them came to blame the disaster not only on the Army leadership that was immediately responsible for carrying on the war, but also on the civilian rulers who had led Bolivia into the conflict in the first place. They began to question the whole social, economic, and political system, which they conceived had made possible such a bloody defeat" (1982, p. 66).

With the stimulus to nationalism and self-identity provided by the war, the national and new petty bourgeoisie began a political assault against the *rosca* in a series of reformist governments (notably that of Villarroel). The MNR was formed by individuals of this class and represented the interests and corresponding nationalist ideology accordingly. During the same postwar period, the peasants who had served as the foot soldiers returned to the unchanged hacienda system of coerced labor.[6] The *campesinos* returned from the war with a perspective that, like that of the young officers, was greatly changed by their wartime mobilization. The *campesinos* were ready to view themselves in a new political context—one that would promise political equality and property rights to the land they worked.

Peasantry—National Indigenous Congress

In late 1943 and early 1944, under the initiative of *campesino* leaders such as Ramos Quevedo, the National Indigenous Committee was organized under the auspices of the Gualberto Villarroel government (see below). The committee consisted of about 15 peasant representatives from around the country. It rapidly forged a network of contacts with local leaders in the communities and haciendas. Even with the national governments sanction, local meetings were often deemed unacceptable by the hacendados. Campesino "ringleaders" and "agitators" were frequently expelled from the haciendas and jailed or physically abused with the consent of the local authorities. Despite this persecution, the committee was able to develop the kind of supra-local organization that the hacendados had been careful to repress in the past (Dandler and Torrico 1987, pp. 347–48).

Despite harassment by local officials and media accounts defaming the "dangerous agitators," the National Indigenous Congress was held in La Paz in May 1945. The government-approved decrees that resulted from the convergence attempted to deal directly with relations of production rather than land ownership. The Congress-Villarroel decrees were directed at eliminating the personal services of *pongueaje* and *mitanage* and limiting the kinds of services the hacendado could be allowed to extract from the *colonos*. Among other things the decrees declared that the *colono* was the absolute owner of his harvest and may sell it freely; tributes may not be exacted by proprietors for free, or as remuneration under the heading of cattle herbage and pasturing fees (see Dandler and Torrico 1987, p. 353).

Even before Villarroel's assassination, the national government was unable to enforce these decrees. In fact, the Villarroel government itself had, at an August 1945 Congress of Hacendados, presented the case for defining the obligations of the peasants as a measure to maintain order, "to avert the advance of an indigenous revolt, encouraged and instigated by political elements adverse to the current regime" (*La Razón,* August 17, 1945; cited in Dandler and Torrico 1987, p. 360). In any event, after the death of Villarroel, the peasants were defenseless. The hacendados declared the Villarroel decrees nonexistent and brutally repressed a succession of peasant uprisings (Dandler and Torrico 1987, p. 361).

The Miners—Thesis of Pulacayo

In November 1946, four months after the fall of the Villarroel-MNR regime, the FSTMB held an extraordinary congress at the southern mining town of Pulacayo under conditions of rising repression and a strong right-wing backlash. Two of the POR's most active militants, Guillermo Lora (a delegate for the miners at Siglo XX) and Fernando Bravo (a correspondent for the conservative newspaper *El Diario*), attended the congress. Despite confusion at the conference, abetted by Lechin's "double and prevarications," Lora and Bravo were able to write Lechin's radical speech and to gain support for an extensive political resolution (Dunkerley 1984, p. 17).

Labeled the Thesis of Pulacayo, the resolution applied Trotsky's 1938 Transitional Program to Bolivian conditions with special reference to trade union objectives. It defined Bolivia as a backward capitalist country, identified the proletariat as the only truly revolutionary class, called for an alliance under its leadership with peasants, artisans, and the petty bourgeoisie, denounced Stalinism and the *rosca* in equal measure, warned against the dangers in believing in "worker ministers" appointed the bourgeois governments, demanded a sliding scale of wages, occupation of the mines, and a central trade union confederation, and emphasized that the union movement could only have lasting impact if it developed into a working class offensive against capitalism. The document, which became a reference point (albeit often as counterexample to later political choices), may well have disappeared into obscurity had Patiño not had the entire thesis printed in *El Diario* as a warning to the ruling class of the radical nature of the FSTMB (Dunkerley 1984, p. 17).

PREREVOLUTION POLITICS

One of the first political expressions of the national and new petty bourgeoisie was manifested via the military—the "young officers." Not satisfied with the traditional orientation of President José Tejada Sorzano, who had come to the presidency after Salamanca's fall in a 1934 coup, the new group of officers and civilian supporters sponsored the coup of July 1937, which brought Colonel Germán Busch to the presidency. Busch, who later was declared one of the symbols of the Bolivian National Revolution, called elections for a new constitutional assembly.[7] This assembly modified Bolivia's constitution and elected

Busch as constitutional president. Regardless, Busch dissolved congress in April 1939 and declared himself a dictator.

The notable aspect of Busch's government was its move against the *rosca*. Busch issued the country's first labor code, nationalized the Banco Central and Banco Minero (the major financial institution for the mining industry), and proclaimed that the mining companies had to sell all foreign exchange to the Central Bank. These policies held wide popular support, but were opposed by the mining company owners—particularly the "big three": Patiño, Aramayo, and Hothschild. On August 23, 1939, Busch either committed suicide or was murdered. Upon his death, General Carlos Quintanilla was placed in the presidency; he quickly acted to reverse those measures that Busch had directed against the private mining interests. Later in 1939, General Enrique Peñaranda, supported by the *rosca*, replaced Quintanilla.

Formation of Political Parties

Despite the ascendancy of the *rosca*'s control over state policy, various political parties, each with the goal of fundamental change, formed in the late 1930s and 1940s. These parties were the Falange Socialista Boliviana (FSB), the Partido de Izquierda Revolucionario (PIR), the Partido Obrero Revolucionario (POR), and the MNR (Alexander 1982, p. 68). The FSB was established in 1937, by a group of exiled Bolivians residing in Chile, as a fascist-oriented party, patterned on the Spanish Falange of José Antonio Primo de Rivera. Constituted principally of intellectuals with some contacts among Bolivian military officers, it remained a small party until shortly after the 1952 revolution, when it became the principal right-wing opposition to the revolutionary government.

The POR was formed in 1934, by the Túpac Amaru group, as part of Trotsky's Fourth International. The Túpac Amarus had been established by exiles in Argentina during the Chaco War under the leadership of Gustavo Navarro (or Tristán Marof). Following his return to Bolivia, Navarro was accused of opportunism by the POR leadership and was replaced by José Aguirre Gainsborg. Gainsborg died in an accident in 1938, and Guillermo Lora emerged as the principal figure in the POR by the end of the 1940s. The POR (as well as the MNR) gained major support from the miners in the decade previous to the revolution.

The PIR was a Stalinist party established in 1940 as the result of a conference of representatives of a number of small left-wing groups made up mostly of intellectuals. Its principal leader in the 1940s was José Antonio Arce, a sociologist and professor at the University of San Andres in La Paz. Other important figures in the PIR included Ricardo Anaya of the University of Cochabamba and novelist Jesús Lara. Most of the leaders of the newly formed national labor confederation, the Confederación Sindical de Trabajadores Bolivianos (CSTB), were members of the PIR, and the party was particularly strong among the railroad workers. Organized in 1941, the MNR was the most important party to appear in the post-Chaco War period. The founders of the party included Victor Paz Estenssoro, Hernán Sile Zuazo, Walter Guevara Arze, and Luis Peñaloza, a one-time member of the Tupac Amarus. In 1940 several of these people had been elected to congress, and after its formal establishment, the MNR became the major critic of the Peñaranda government in parliament (Alexander 1982, pp. 68-70).

These political parties were both catalysts and manifestations of the growing contradictions in Bolivian society that were principally fueled by the increasingly strong urban-based petty bourgeoisie, the radicalized miners, and a discontented peasantry. Over the period of the revolution the divergent interests of these groups were articulated or coalesced into a sufficient political unity that vented itself against the *rosca* in the 1952 revolution. The difficult, if not impossible, task of the political articulation of these groups into a capitalist (or otherwise stable) social formation fell to the MNR. As discussed below, the "democratic" attempt failed by 1964.

MNR and the "Young Officers"

In December 1942 the "Catavi massacre" occurred at the Patiño company's Catavi mine located about 35 miles southeast of Oruro. Pressing for wage increases, the worker's Sindicato de Oficios Various called a strike. Management responded by closing the mine commissary, the workers staged a mass protest march, and a specially dispatched army unit opened fire on the march, killing more than 35 miners. The strike was broken, but the political issue of the Catavi massacre had begun. This evidence of the Peñaranda government's cruelty and subservience to the large mining companies offered clear political advantages to the MNR. However, rather than attempt to mobilize unions and lead a general uprising as it would do in 1952, the MNR planned for a more traditional route to power—the coup d'etat. This plan was implemented through an alliance with a faction of the Bolivian officer corps, which had formed among those held prisoner by the Paraguayans during the Chaco War, called the Razón de Patria (RADEPA) (Mitchell 1977, pp. 20-21).

RADEPA's secret "Minimum Plan of Action" was:

> To govern with the great destitute majority of Bolivians, directing it through a select group of uncontaminated and capable men. . . . To work

intensely under the inspiration of the moto: "Bolivia for the Bolivians, without exploited or exploiters." To assure for the collective the enormous riches in our soil, controlling production, exports, and imports; combatting international exploitation and specualtion. . . . To put an end to the anarchy which consumes us, reconstructing the national soul and creating pride in Bolivianism, basing itself on the glories of our national history and tradition, rooted in the greatness of the Inca empire and the antecedents of our Indian race. . . (in Mitchell 1977, p. 22).

These proposals were obviously indicative of the group's nationalist idealism. Significantly, it should be noted that the document traces or roots the concept of the Bolivian nation in the history of the Indian. It is also true that the document clearly indicates the fascist tone of at least some elements of the RADEPA. This mixture of the right-wing and the left-wing inside the MNR after that party's alliance with RADEPA is one explanation of the MNR's later factionalism and failure as a ruling political party.

In 1943 RADEPA and the MNR formed an alliance and agreed to cooperate in the overthrow of Peñaranda. On December 20, 1943, RADEPA members seized command of important regiments while the MNR took control of the telephone system and armed La Paz traffic police patrolled the city in the name of a new government. Major Gualberto Villarroel of RADEPA became president and remained in office until his death by hanging at the hands of a disgruntled mob in front of the presidential palace in July 1946.

Although Paz Estenssoro was an influential advisor to Villarroel during the two and one-half years of his rule, the MNR was of secondary importance to the military leadership. Many officers within RADEPA suspected the MNR members of being too radical, and the party's influence often depended upon the personal support of the "quiet, scholarly, and administrative-minded Villarroel" (Mitchell 1977, p. 22). Mitchell argues that during this period the MNR moved toward a populist strategy perhaps in some part as a response to its weakness relative to the military. In any case, the MNR acted to capture the political support of the labor movement and supported the formation of a strong national miner's union. Although the miners had been politically active in some mines for nearly 50 years, they were not able to organize at the national level. However, in June 1944 efforts to organize culminated in a congress of 30 delegates, claiming to represent as many as 60,000 miners. The delegates met in the mining town of Huanuni and created the Federación Sindical de Trabajadores Mineros de Bolivia (FSTMB). An MNR ally (if not a member), Juan Lechin Oquendo, became the union's executive secretary. Lechin retained this position until the mid-1980s. Along with Paz and Siles, Lechin became a major fixture in the modern period of Bolivian politics.

The MNR leadership also began to look tentatively to the peasantry for political backing. In the 1944 constitutional convention, Paz and Guevara Arze introduced the following article dealing with land reform:

> Peasants who lack land or do not have enough for their needs, have the right to be given land in the same region. To this end we declare the necessity and public utility of expropriations of necessary land, following indemnification (in Mitchell 1977, p. 23).

Little action resulted from the MNR's call for land reform and, although the MNR endorsed the first peasant congress, which was attended by 1,000 peasant representatives in 1945, the MNR did not act to mobilize the peasantry as did the PIR and the POR (Mitchell 1977, p. 24).

Politics to the Revolution

The ruling front that took power following Villarroel's death held elections in January 1947. Enrique Hertzog of the Partido de Unificación Republicana Socialista (PURS) won, narrowly defeating the Liberal candidate. Malloy maintains that the PURS, though identified by the MNR as being allied with the Liberals as a united oligarchy, saw itself as an enlightened elite determined to salvage the system through limited reform. The Villarroel constitution was abrogated, but its replacement differed only in detail and contained the same economic and social principles current since Busch. Nonetheless, the pressure was at least partially removed from the mine companies as many of the acts favoring labor were ignored. The PURS administrations of Hertzog and his successor, Mamerto Urriolagoitia, constantly seemed to be taking public pro-labor, antimine owner positions, and then being pressured by the owners into public capitulation (Malloy 1970, pp. 128–30).

During the "sexino"—the six years from 1946 to the revolution—the MNR moved to expand its political base by continuing to court the working class. In early 1947 most of the MNR members who had fled or gone into hiding upon the fall of Villarroel came into the open and "began plotting with anyone available and using every opportunity to foment social unrest." The PURS responded to the MNR activities as well as to labor actions not incited by the MNR with erratic violence and accusations of MNR rabble rousing. In effect, as Malloy points out, the PURS acted as a publicity agent for the MNR among the miners (1970, p. 133). "The end result was the rise of the MNR once again to a preeminent position. Removing its more profascist elements and absorbing the most important labor supporters of the Trotskyist POR, the MNR became a powerful middle and working class movement of socialist reform and the leading opponent of the rule of the traditional elite" (Kelley and Klein 1981, p. 94).

Immediately previous to the 1951 elections, the PURS attempted to win the votes of the miners by requiring the owners to provide a 30-percent increase in wages. The owners openly defied the PURS and threatened to reduce wages if the PURS continued to demand the increase. Consequently, the PURS entered the elections with no credibility to its claim of being independent of the *rosca*. At the same time the MNR received the support of the POR and the newly formed Partido Comunista de Bolivia (PCB). Paz and Siles headed the MNR ticket as presidential and vice-presidential candidates, respectively.

The MNR won a plurality, polling 54,049 votes. The PURS was second with 39,940 votes; the Liberal party acquired only 6,441 votes. As would be expected from the analysis of the structural changes of which the MNR was the primary political indication, the MNR carried all the active, "national" areas of Bolivia—La Paz, Cochabamba, Oruro, and Potosí (1970, p. 153). Because the MNR had not received a majority, the election was to be decided by congress. Fearing that congress would confer victory on the MNR, the mine owners supported a military coup, which resulted in the presidency of General Hugo Ballivián. As might be expected from the vote totals of the aborted election and the increasingly radical position of the miners, this government could not contain the forces representative of the emerging social configuration. Within one year from the coup the Bolivian National Revolution occurred.

REVOLUTION AND OUTCOMES

In April 1952, after three days of heavy street fighting in La Paz in which armed groups of municipal police, tin miners, and other civilians battled and defeated the army of Bolivia, the MNR gained control. Some 600 people were killed in the fighting as MNR civilians seized the national armories and distributed the weapons to their supporters. Miners from the Milluni mine seized the railroad station on the slope above La Paz while other miners blocked possible government reinforcements from leaving Oruro. With armed miners above the city and rebels controlling the center, the capital troops were trapped. On April 11 the MNR established itself as the ruling political party of Bolivia (Malloy 1970, p. 157). The MNR jailed or exiled most of the officer corp, distributed arms to the populace, and within five days had established its own military

Postrevolutionary Bolivian Politics 69

organization composed of armed worker and civilian militia (see Alexander 1982).

Encompassing the support of the three major groups of the newly articulated Bolivian social formation, the MNR—with Paz Estenssoro in the presidency—was primarily and perhaps inevitably an actor for the interests of the new petty bourgeoisie. In any event, the demands of the insurgent miners for nationalization of the mining industry had to be met. The new government created a state monopoly over mineral exports in July and then nationalized the three big tin producers in October, organizing them into the state mining company of (COMIBOL). With the government oil monopoly (YPFB) and the state development corporation (CBF), both established before the revolution, the takeover of the mines made the state the single largest producer of goods and services in the nation and the single largest employer (Kelley and Klein 1981, p. 94).

By some accounts, rural land reform may never have been inaugurated by the MNR if not for the growing mobilization of the peasantry. Clearly, though, the MNR intended, in some manner, to incorporate the peasantry into the national economy. In Hernán Siles Suazo's first speech at the conclusion of the revolution, he called for "effort and calm" and went on to speak of the construction of a new Bolivia: "We are going to work so that the Bolivian economy belongs to Bolivians and not the exploiters who live abroad. We are going to incorporate the *campesinos* into the Bolivian economy and national life so that they are no longer the objects of derision" (in Dunkerley 1984, p. 41). The MNR did not have a clear program for the countryside. Generally, however, the argument or situation mandating land reform became twofold. First, many of the urban-based supporters of the revolution saw the hacienda system of agricultural production as inefficient. Second, the peasantry, if not given its own land through a system of land redistribution, seemed to be on the verge of revolt.

According to Kelley and Klein, the peasants used their traditional community organizations as the basis of formal union, or *sindicato,* organizations and were able to mobilize rapidly to become the dominant military force in the campo. From April 1952 to the middle of 1953, armed peasants systematically destroyed the old hacienda system. Comparing their actions to the "Great Fear" period of the French Revolution, Kelley and Klein note "the Bolivian peasants burned work records, killed or harassed landowners, and in short order forced the old elite into exile in the capital or abroad" (Kelley and Klein 1981, p. 95). With moderates and radicals within and without the MNR disagreeing on the actual form and extent of agrarian reform, actual enactment was a foregone conclusion by early 1953.

The presence of a mobilized peasantry may or may not have struck fear in those holding a "moderate" position within the MNR. From a "moderate" point of view the presence of a mobilized peasantry supplemented the plans of the MNR for extending capitalism to the countryside. As Javier Albó and Josep Barnadas point out the pre-1953 hacendados were politically linked to the mine owners, composing the *"rosca minero-feudal"* (1985, p. 236). In opposition to this entire bloc, the MNR had no political justification to support the land owners. Rather, the general and agreed upon objective was to expand the political base of the state to include the *campesinado*. If only from political pragmatism, such a policy was wise in view of the fact that (with their newly granted suffrage) the peasantry represented the single largest potential voting bloc in future elections. This political objective was supported ideologically as well. The objective flowed logically from the nationalism that the MNR represented as expressed in such documents as in the above cited RADEPA statement.

In January 1953 the government established a commission to study and propose an agrarian reform plan. This was done in response to, and in the context of, peasant union demonstrations of power. In the Lake Titicaca and Cochabamba valley areas, *campesinos* acted to obstruct urban-rural trade. In February 1953 armed peasants temporarily entered the main plaza and downtown area in the city of Cochabamba to protest government attempts to stop the unionization movement. By August 1953, when Paz decreed agrarian reform at a ceremony in a politically active rural village of Cochabamba, de facto land redistribution had already occurred in many areas of Bolivia. Even after the 1953 decree, the peasant unions' policy was to encourage extralegal (or extrabureaucratic) land seizure. So forceful was this that by the mid-1950s there were no longer any traditional landlords and hacendados in much of the major indigenous peasant areas (Kelley and Klein 1981, p. 96).

Not all peasants benefited from the reform. Some already owned their land and others lived in isolated areas where the hacendados were able to evade land reform. Data indicate that by 1955 approximately 45 percent of all rural families had benefited from the reform (Wilkie 1974, p. 3; cited in Kelley and Klein 1981, p. 97). "After two years 51 percent of the latifundia in La Paz, 49 percent in Chuquisaca, and 76 percent in Oruro had been affected . . . in Tarija the figure was 33 percent, in Santa Cruz 36 percent, and in Cochabamba only 16 percent, the national total being 28.5 percent" (Dunkerley 1984, p. 73). These figures, being the measure of land that was processed through the bureaucracy, do not reflect the land that was seized directly by the peasants and not legally ratified until much later, if at all. This would explain the low figure for Cochabamba. The low Santa Cruz figure can be explained by the fact that the region contained farms that were protected by the agrarian reform decree under the category of "agricultural enterprise." In any case, the data on property size show that the peasant generally broke off or claimed for himself only a small portion of the hacienda that he had been working. "In 1959 agricultural property in the department of La Paz was divided into 64,280 separate units, of which 45,281 were less than one hectare in size" (Dunkerley 1984, p. 74). This "minifundisimo" was not an intentional policy of the MNR. Yet, the phenomenon of minifundisimo was a result of two general factors. One, the peasants of former haciendas generally did not leave their hacienda. That is, haciendas were split among the former *"colonos"* who were not compelled to leave that land. Secondly, and the explanation for the first factor, the peasants were not, after all, capitalist by legal decree. Leaving the land they had worked to acquire larger plots elsewhere for the sake of producing profit for reinvestment was not part of the peasants' ideology.[8]

For the MNR, the peasantry proved itself an effective counter to the demands placed on the state by the miners. Conflict between the MNR government and the labor movement increased steadily and inevitably. The Confederación Obrero Boliviano (COB), led by the miners, won concessions on wages, subsidized stores for miners, and inefficiently high levels of labor employment in the mines. This, combined with the low quality of the remaining ores, decapitalization of the mines, and weak world market for tin, resulted in huge losses for the government mining company. Out of economic necessity (from management's point of view) and, somewhat later, from international pressure in the form of the Triangular Plan, the government acted to break the power of the miners. The peasantry was a ready partner or, perhaps more aptly, a client of the state when political and military suppression of the miners was required. With the hacienda system destroyed, peasant *sindicatos* favored no further fundamental changes such as those being proposed by minority elements within the MNR of forming rural production collectives. By offering some public works projects, such as roads and schools, the national government was able to secure *campesino* cooperation. In La Paz, for example, when faced with opposition or attempted coups, the government would invite thousands of armed *campesinos* from the altiplano into the city on a few hours notice (Kelley and Klein 1981, pp. 101–2).

For reasons of political expedience the MNR did not attempt to intervene in the economic reorganization of the countryside other than to oversee the parcellization of private property. By default, MNR agrarian policy was based on the theory that the transformation of peasants into holders of small properties would transform them into "farmers." The planners relied, in effect, upon "market forces" to bring the peasantry into the capitalist economy as producers and consumers (see Albó & Barnadas 1985, p. 235). By the mid-1980s, this policy was viewed by most policymakers as having failed (see ILDIS, *Debates Agrarias*).

POSTREFORM PEASANT-STATE POLITICS

From 1952 to 1964, civilian government was maintained in Bolivia through a series of four-year administrations of Paz, Siles, and Paz. Throughout this period the *campesinado* as a whole supported the Bolivian state as the MNR leadership acted to consolidate the position of capital vis-a-vis labor particularly in the single major industrial sector—tin mining. Also during this period, both Paz and Siles acted to reconstruct the Bolivian military and disband the civil militia. Capitalist development in Bolivia remained weak, with an economy that relied upon the export of tin and (until the development of oil and natural gas production) little else.

A substantial portion of the newly freed labor supply from the *campo* found occupation in merchant activities such as the smuggling of small consumer goods from neighboring countries and marketing them from city sidewalks. Another portion entered the cities as salaried domestic work, or as vendors of small goods or services. Another portion began the patterns of seasonal migration—first to northern Argentina, then to the Santa Cruz region (and later, in the 1980s to the coca producing regions of the Chapare). At the same time, in an attempt to spur capitalist development, the country was made receptive to foreign investment and the economic policies suggested by international agencies. This policy was constantly challenged and was a source of the fragmentation of the MNR.[9]

The *campesinado* proved to be the stabilizing or, at least, a reliably constant factor until the mid-1970s, constituting the majority of the population. No national government was willing to implement policy that might upset the traditional life and economy of the *campesinado* and thereby antagonize that group. To a large degree, government policy toward the peasantry was based on the idea that agriculture products from the indigenous areas simply were not significant enough as a national income source to merit actions (i.e., action to force production for the marketplace) that could risk alienating the necessary political support of the peasantry. No moves were openly contemplated to promote capitalist development in the zones where the *campesinado* held political power because such moves would be perceived by the peasantry as threatening to their existence. Little or no resources were used, then, to increase the production capacity of the land over which the indigenous farmers retained jealous control. In areas where the *campesinado* was not well organized, such as in the Chuquisaca region, quasi-feudal relations of production were allowed to persist (see Healy 1979). In other areas where the *campesinado* was not well organized mainly because the *indio* did not exist qua peasant, such as in the Santa Cruz region, the establishment of capitalist agricultural did receive attention as those areas were opened to commerce with the rest of Bolivia as well as to Brazil and Argentina.

Nonetheless, Bolivia, as a national entity, was composed mostly of peasants (i.e., subsistence agriculturalists who lived mostly on the altiplano and in the few principal Andean valleys). In the mid-1980s about 55 percent of all Bolivians were involved in agriculture. Eighty percent of those Bolivians lived on the altiplano and in the valleys (Zagha 1984, p. 2). It is the politics of the campesinos of these regions to which we turn next. The following examination of the political history of the organized *campesinado* is intended to anticipate the structural explanation of change in Bolivia that is presented in the next chapter.

The most significant *campesinado* movement of the mid-1980s was the Confederación Sindical Unica Trabajadores Campesinado de Bolivia (CSUTCB). In the 1980s this organization was headed by Genaro Flores, who came to the leadership of the CSUTCB from a background of involvement in the indigenous political movement known as *katarismo*. The existence of the CSUTCB was a result of the postrevolutionary resurgence of *indigenismo*. As demonstrated in the previous chapter, *indigenismo* had been a recurring feature in Bolivian history. The modern renewal of it adopted the label *katarismo* from an Aymaran rebel of the colonial period, Túpac Katari.[10]

Katarismo as a modern movement was traced by Javier Hurtado (1986) to a group of Aymaran students at the secondary school Gaulberto Villarroel in La Paz in the 1960s. This group of students began a study of Bolivian history from the perspective of the indigenous population. Under the leadership of Raymundo Tambo these students formed a clandestine study group, which became known as the *Movimiento 15 de Noviembre*. Hurtado maintains (and the later documents of the CSUTCB support the thesis) that this movement, though obviously wanting to emphasize the role of the *indio* in Bolivia, did not carry with it the racist baggage in which such a perspective could perhaps too easily pack itself.

In 1962 Fausto Reinaga, a historian and writer on the Bolivian *indio*, founded the Partido indio aymara kechua, which was later shortened to the name Partido indio de Bolivia (PIB). In contrast to the November group, Reinaga's writings and party reflected his racial (or racist) glorification of the Bolivian Indian.[11] However, in 1968 the executive committee of this party was reorganized and members of the *15 de Noviembre* group were elected to that body, thus combining the two currents; one giving the indigenous struggle a racial emphasis and the other viewing "the problem of the *campesinado* from a national and class perspective." These two currents split in 1978. The racial current formed the party Movimiento indio Tupaj Katari (MITKA) under the leadership of Constatino Lima. The other current formed the Movimiento Revolucionario Tupaj Katari (MRTKA) under the leadership of Flores (Hurtado, 1986, pp. 32–33).

This development took place on a background of military dictatorship. In 1964, upon the reelection of Paz to a third term in office, the vice-presidential candidate, General René Barrientos, staged a military insurrection and took power. Previous to 1964, Barrientos was active in the affairs of the campesino unions. Whereas Paz relied upon a strategy of dividing the competing groups within the *campesinado*, Barrientos had the disputing *campesino* leaders to his residence in La Paz, had them agree to settle their differences peacefully, and support him as the vice-presidential candidate in 1964 (Dunkerley 1984, p. 116). At the time of the insurrection, the established campesino organization, the Confederación Nacional Trabajadores Campesinado de Bolivia (CNTCB), remained a willing collaborator of the state against the miners. Barrientos' ability to speak Quechua, his pride in being a *"cochabambino,"* and his "charisma" allowed him to maintain a special relationship with the *campesinado*. This relationship came to be referred to as the *"pacto militar-campesinado."*

After Barrientos' death in a helicopter crash in 1969, Luis Adolfo Siles Salinas, a Social Democrat who had been officially elected vice president in 1966, occupied the presidency for a few months. Siles Salinas was kidnapped and forced into exile and General Alfredo Ovando followed him into the presidency. Ovando, who had been instrumental in the success of the Barrientos insurrection, led a nationalist faction of the army and moved the government somewhat to the Left. Most notably, he appointed the famed and later martyred leader of the Partido Socialista Uno (PS-1), Marcelo Quiroga Santa Cruz, minister of hydrocarbons. Quiroga, with the support of General Juan José Torres, moved to nationalize the Bolivian holdings of the Gulf Oil company. This action was made official by Ovando in late 1969. Besides nationalization of Gulf, Ovando established relations and commercial treaties with the Soviet Union, Rumania, Hungary, and Czechoslovakia, and re-legalized parties on the Left (Dunkerley 1984, 166–67).

The Ovando regime was inevitably weakened by the conservatives and those in the military who wished to maintain the privileges of the positions they held under Barrientos. In the actual clash in 1970, between Ovando and the Right, the same Juan Jose Torres who had supported Quiroga in the nationalization of Gulf Oil stepped into power with support from the air force, but most importantly,

Postrevolutionary Bolivian Politics 75

with support from the COB and the *Comando Politico* (Dunkerley 1984, p. 177).

The Torres regime was never able to consolidate its support from the worker's movement and the Left into a base of support capable of withstanding a backlash from the Right. Following a series of events that aroused the ire of the military, Colonels Hugo Banzer Suarez and Edmundo Valencia attempted a coup that was defeated by a general strike in January 1971. Torres moved further to the Left to maintain and gain further support from the workers. A number of factors acted against Torres, however; including the Nixon administration's move to sell off U.S. stockpiles of tin and to prevent loans to Bolivia from the Inter-American Development Bank. In August 1971 Banzer was able to successfully stage a coup against the Torres regime. And so began the "Banzarato" (Dunkerley 1984, pp. 179–200).

During Banzer's regime from 1971 until July 1978, there were a minimum of 200 people killed (excluding those killed during the takeover). Some 14,750 people were jailed for "offenses against the state," a further 19,140 were forced into political exile, and some 780,000 people became economic refugees. Throughout this period there was no independent union activity, no freedom to participate in politics, and the press was strictly censored. Even some of the MNR membership, which had been brought into Banzer's Frente Popular Nacionalista (FPN) alliance, were arrested and tortured (Dunkerley 1984, p. 208).

The special relationship of support between the military and the *campesinado* lasted through the death of Barrientos and into the administration of General Banzer. However, in 1974 at the massacre of Tolata and Espizana, the special relationship began its collapse. In response to a government announcement of a new policy regarding food prices, *campesinos* and workers throughout Bolivia began protest demonstrations. In the Department of Cochabamba, protests began on January 22 with workers from the Manaco shoe factory in Quillacollo. Between January 24 and January 30, about 20,000 *campesinos* occupied and blocked the highways that linked Cochabamba with Santa Cruz, the Chapare, Oruro, and Sucre. The center of the movement was located in the villages of Tolata and Epizana on the highway to Santa Cruz. Used to the patronizing actions of Barrientos, the *campesinos* demanded and expected to meet with Banzer personally at the blockade. Instead, they met with artillery fire and strafing in a military in Tolata and Epizana on the 29th. Military action continued the next day in other provinces of Cochabamba and the province of Aroma (the home village of many of those active in the *katarista* movement) in La Paz (Rivera 1984, pp. 135–36).

From that event (and the repressive measures implemented by Banzer in November 1974) the *campesinado* began an immediate departure from its politics of cooperation with the military. The *katarista* movement, heading this shift, first worked to penetrate the government controlled Confederación Nacional de Trabajadores Campesinos de Bolivia (CNTCB) and then established the CSUTCB as a counter organization under the leadership of Flores (who, as mentioned above, was also leader of the MRTK) during a brief "democratic opening" in 1979.

The Banzer regime had been pressured by domestic dissent and coercion from the United States to move toward elections. With General Juan Pereda as the handpicked candidate of the military, the election was held in July 1978. However, the blatant nature of the electoral fraud that was committed to ensure a win for Pereda prevented the military from claiming a legitimate victory. Pereda solved the problem in the short-term by staging a coup against Banzer that forced his resignation. Unable to maintain the support of the military or the civilian forces that had aided him in the overthrow of Banzer, Pereda was himself forced out by the military in November 1978 and replaced by General David Padilla Arancibia. Arancibia represented the view of those in the military that political power had to be handed to civilian authority if only to build the institutional or professional reputation of the military. His government went so far as to initiate legal action against Banzer for the Tolata massacre. Though this action was dropped in the face of growing antimilitarist sentiment, new elections were scheduled for and held in July 1979 (Dunkerley 1984, pp. 254–55).

Many of the political parties, such as Hernán Siles Zuazo's Unidad Democrática Popular (UDP) (which was an umbrella party composed of several parties of the center Left and notably of one faction of the MRTK), had become active for the 1978 election. An important addition to the 1979 race was the new party—Acción Democrática Nacionalista (ADN)—formed by the now civilian Hugo Banzer. The UDP won a plurality of the popular vote with 592,886 votes but with this only gained 46 seats in both houses of the national Bolivian Congress. Because of the distribution of districts, the Alianza-MNR (AMNR)—an umbrella grouping of parties of the center Right and the pro-Moscow Partido Comunista Leninista (PCML) by Victor Paz's MNR—with a popular vote total of 539,744 gained 54 seats in congress. Hugo Banzer's ADN gained 225,205 popular votes and 21 seats in congress. None of these groups wished to form a governing alliance with either of the other groups, thus congress was unable to select a president. In the ensuing stalemate, the leader of the senate (or upper chamber), Walter Guevara Arze, was made temporary president until another election could be held in June 1980.

Military hostility toward the civilian government grew as the congress debated measures to placate the International Monetary Fund, which was pressuring the regime to make payments on the foreign debt that had incurred during the Banzerato. The parties of the Left (and the COB) and those of the Right could not agree on, much less sustain, a coherent economic policy. On November 1, 1979, Colonel Alberto Natusch Busch staged a military coup by moving a tank corp into the streets of La Paz. Opposition to the coup from all sectors, including the ADN, did not discourage Natusch at least for the first week. In what is actually a rarity in Bolivian coups, Natusch sought to coerce cooperation with the actual use of military violence in the streets. Before he was finally convinced to end his attempt at governing 14 days after the coup, over 200 citizens were dead, 200 were wounded, and 125 were disappeared (Dunkerley 1984, p. 267).

Through negotiations with the civilian leadership, the military agreed to withdraw after extracting the guarantee that Guevara would not return to the presidency. The leader of the lower house, Lidia Gueiler Tejada, became the first woman president of Bolivia coming to the office upon completion of the two-week de facto government of Natusch (which had gained the distinction of being the shortest Bolivian government in power). The Gueiler government presided over a worsening economic situation aided by the fact that some $18 million had disappeared from the vaults of the Banco Central during the Natusch government (Dunkerley 1984, p. 269). The foreign debt exceeded $3 billion, production in agriculture, mining, and oil had fallen by 5.5 percent since 1976. At the same time, public sector expenditure had risen from Bs.8.9 billion in 1976 to an estimated Bs.17.0 billion in 1979. The negative overall growth figure for 1979 was expected to be even greater in 1980, and on its assumption of office the Gueiler government did not have sufficient funds to cover state salaries and running costs for December. In return for the promise of a "standby loan" of $111 million from the IMF, the government announced a 25-percent devaluation of the Bolivian peso and lifted government subsidies on gasoline, oil, and kerosene (the commonly used fuel for cooking) (Dunkerley 1984, p. 273).

Popular reaction in the cities to the implicit tax on the poor that resided in this policy was muted. The leadership of the COB, having accepted the Gueiler government as the alternative to military dictatorship, was not inclined to organize protests against the policy. In contrast, however, the rural population mobilized by the recently formed CSUTCB vociferously protested the policy especially as it affected the cost of transporting their products to market. *Campesinos* moved immediately to seal off the country's main roads and kept produce from going to the cities. Eventually obtaining concessions from the government on an imposed limit on transport costs, and at the urging of the

COB with which it was officially allied, the CSUTCB ended its blockades. In this event, the CSUTCB clearly demonstrated that the *campesinado* was a new force ready to challenge the state. That is, the days of the politics of partnership with the state were finished. In contrast, the event demonstrated that the CSUTCB was not so radical as to, or not politically able to, take on the state without the support of its urban-based partners. Nonetheless, this political alliance with the labor movement (particularly with the miners) marked a dramatic break from the politics of *pacto militar-campesino* (see Hurtado 1986; Rivera 1984).

The CSUTCB came to dominance in the 1980s as the main labor and political force representing the Bolivian *indigena*. Its main strongholds of support were on the altiplano in the departments of La Paz and Potosi (from conversation with Javier Albó, August 1986), but it spoke for and united *campesino sindicatos* from the valleys as well. In that group's 1983 Political Thesis, the CSUTCB identified the "campesinos aymaras, quechuas, cambas, chapacos, chiquitanos, canicnana, itenanmas, cayubas, ayoreodes, tupiwaranies and others" as the "legitimate owners of the land" although they are treated as though dispossessed of the land. This particular document is an excellent example of the ethnic or indigena call to recollection and action. Significantly, though, the document shifts from merely an ethnic appeal. As only a pragmatic consideration by the CSUTCB, a purely ethnic appeal was precluded because the rural population of Bolivia, though mostly Aymara and Quechua, was composed of several groups in the eastern regions that were never part of the Incan social formation. The division between Aymara and Quechua alone could not be ignored by any group claiming to represent the *campesinado*. Though both Aymara and Quechua people were part of the Incan social formation, they have separate languages and histories. No political appeal that hoped to reach the entire native Bolivian population could be based exclusively in one heritage. The obvious ethnic divisions had to be bridged.

The gaps were crossed through the analysis that each group has been oppressed by Spanish colonial domination and the dominant classes of the Republic. Hence the argument became not so much an ethnic appeal as an appeal to a people that have been exploited as a class by the Spanish and the economic system the Spanish brought. The ethnic element was part of this appeal on the basis that the exploited group can identify itself (form a class consciousness of sorts) through the distinction between *indígena* and *blanco*. The contention of the CSUTCB, then, was that the descendants of all the Indian groups "have been converted to second class citizens . . . which is true for most workers in the countryside as well as workers in the cities even though many have lost [through Spanish acculturation] their own cultural roots, but nonetheless are victims of the dominant colonial mentality. Because we are all oppressed we have a common cause of liberation" (CSUTCB 1983: *Tesis Politica,* in Rivera 1984, p. 188).

Among the issues addressed by the CSUTCB was that of rural property tax (which was increased in the package of taxes announced in 1986). Another issue was that of government or Banco Agricola Boliviano (BAB) agricultural credit policies. The 1986 CSUTCB document argued that the government, through the use of variable interest loans, raised interest on loans from 84% to 792%. A figure that, of course, reflected the tremendous inflation that Bolivia experienced between 1983 and 1986. The consequence of this inflation and high interest rates was the conversion of the borrowers into salaried "peones" of the new private landholders (section from the Economic Commission of the CSUTCB thesis 1983).

At the national political level, the CSUTCB's development had to contend with the repressive military regime of General Luis Garcia Meza, which came to power in July 1980 through a coup d'etat against the government of Lidia Gueiler Tejada, which had presided over the promised elections of June 1980. Although still not resulting in a majority of congressional seats for the UDP, the June 29 election gave 53 seats to the UDP compared to 40 seats to the second place AMNR. Banzer's ADN gained 25 seats with nearly as many popular votes as those garnered by the AMNR—220,309 and 263,706, respectively. With 507,173 votes for the UDP, Siles once again was able to claim the clear popular mandate. The new congress met and voted for Siles as president to be inaugurated August 6, 1980. The inauguration would have to wait until October 1982.

Garcia Meza, chief of military in the Gueiler administration, staged a rebellion on July 17 from the city of Trinidad. His action was supported in the city of La Paz by Arce Gomez who began by leading paramilitary personnel to capture the labor and Left party leaders who, as members of the Comite Nacionale de Defensa de la Democracia (CONADE), were meeting at COB headquarters to discuss measures to counter the brewing military coup. The FSTMB leader Gualberto Vega and Carlos Flores, a leader of a faction of the POR, were shot dead during the assault. As the remaining 36 CONADE members were marched out, Marcelo Quiroga Santa Cruz (who was then leader of Partido Socialista Uno, PS-1) was separated out and shot on the spot. The others, including Juan Lechin Oquendo, were taken prisoner. As other political leaders, including Siles, heard the news of the raid and escaped the city and fled into exile, Gueiler was taken from the palace by the rebels and forced to sign her resignation (1984, pp. 288-89). On July 22 Lechin appeared on television in apparent mental and physical exhaustion to declare, "We can talk over our problems and ambitions some other day, but let us now avoid useless bloodshed. I repeat: I exhort all workers and *campesinos* and the people in general to abandon blockades and civil resistance" (in Dunkerley 1984, p. 290). Except for the miners, civil resistance to the coup collapsed by the end of July after some 30 deaths, and the taking of at least 500 prisoners (Dunkerley 1984, p. 290).

The Garcia Meza regime is probably best known for its alliance with the cocaine mafia and its move to directly profit from the cocaine trade. It should also be remembered for its organization and use of the Servicio Especial de Seguridad (SES), which roamed the streets nightly during the quiet hours of curfew in vehicles marked as ambulances to dispatch with those critical of the regime. Even the Reagan administration in the United States could not justify reinstating the economic aid that President Jimmy Carter had cut off upon the Garcia Meza coup (for which Carter was labeled a communist and enemy of the Bolivian nation). Without U.S. aid or a coherent economic policy, the Garcia Meza regime was subject to the escalating fiscal problems that had affected its immediate predecessors. Garcia Meza proved, in effect, that it was impossible to sustain a right-wing government on anti-U.S. policies for any length of time. Although revenue from the cocaine trade was substantial and facilitated the funding of a sizeable informal apparatus of control, the purchase of loyalty in the upper echelons of the military, and the accumulation of impressive personal fortunes, it could not compensate for the collapse of the legal economy, service the foreign debt, or finance state operations over a sustained period of time (Dunkerley 1984, p. 293).

The problem of U.S. aid was solved in July 1981 when Colonel Natusch Busch staged a coup against the regime from the city of Santa Cruz by shutting off the flow of oil and gas from the Oriente to the highlands. After a standoff of a little more than a week, Natusch ended the coup in exchange for the resignation of Garcia Meza. With power handed to a military junta of Waldo Bernal, Celso Torrelio, and Oscar Pammo, the Reagan administration resumed aid to the Bolivian government.[12]

By September 1981 Celso Torrelio emerged as the de facto president. In July 1982 power was handed to General Guido Vildoso, who oversaw the return of power in October that year to the government that had been elected through the June 1980 electoral process. At the helm of a bankrupt economy, Siles Suazo suspended payment on the foreign debt and declared all private debts (contracted in dollars) payable in Bolivian pesos. With a fixed rate of exchange, bankers and others in a position to demand dollars from the government at the official price were able to reap huge profits as the real value of the peso declined sharply. At the same time, the COB and especially the FSTMB called frequent general strikes to protest sinking real wages. With the economy and political situation crumbling, Siles stepped down a year early from his term of office and elections were held in July 1985. As in the case of the 1979 elections, no party was able to gain a clear congressional majority (or sustain a claim for a popular mandate). This time, however, Banzer's ADN party agreed to support Paz (who had been making much the same campaign statements as Banzer in any case) and who was then inaugurated president in August 1985.

CONCLUSION

In the mid-1980s Bolivia faced perhaps the worst economic crisis of any time. President Paz Estenssoro, who returned to the presidency in August 1985 for the fourth time since 1952, kept political unrest to a minimum. He accomplished this by acting swiftly to detain union leaders when strikes and demonstrations had been planned. However, his political ability to do this, especially as a president during a "democratic opening," was contingent upon the overall weakening of the labor movement, the COB. The debilitation of the COB was caused by the same immediate reason for the general crisis. That is, the large decline in the market price of tin and the inability of the Bolivian tin mines to produce at a cost beneath that price has dramatically affected the tin-dependent economy. In October 1985 the price of tin fell to half its price (Crabtree 1987, p. 4). By August 1986 the total number of miners had fallen to 19,000. One third of the miners employed by the government mining company (COMIBOL)—formed after nationalization in 1952—had either left or been removed from their jobs (Crabtree 1987, pp. 18–19). If it can be said that the COB was radical in outlook and action, it was because it was led by the radicalized miner's union, the FSTMSB. Tin mining, the successor to the silver mining, which declined in the nineteenth century, had been Bolivia's single largest source of foreign exchange, constituting about one third of total exports in the late 1970s from over one half in the early 1970s (Banco Central de Bolivia, cited in Crabtree 1987, p. 69). More importantly, it was the single industry in Bolivia that depended upon a large wage-labor force. Given the terrible working conditions of the mines, "exploitation" was not an analytical abstraction, but a concrete reality experienced by the workers in a context where the private owners (and later the state) were a clearly identifiable class (or representatives of a class) of exploiters. Where a peasant may not know the reason for his or her poverty and may not have a ready view of the "oppressor," a factory worker or miner can easily recognize that profit is made from his or her labor and (in this case at least) damaged body.

It is not surprising that the miners were ready to frame their demands in the terms of class struggle and became the soldiers of the revolutionary coalition during the week of violent struggle in La Paz in April 1952. However, this radicalism was largely restricted to the miners. Bolivia did not develop a significant industrial sector; and a "working class," as such, did not emerge generally in Bolivia. The unions, or *sindicatos,* of the workers and peasants that did form were intentionally structured to be part of a "corporatist" society. This "syndicalism" created a hierarchical structure of administration within the various unions, which lent itself to an uneasy clientelism between government and union leaders.

Paz Estenssoro was effective in quelling opposition to his policies because, first, the labor movement in Bolivia was not such that the "rank-and-file workers" of the city or countryside rose to the defense of the COB leadership. Second, the radical minority of the labor movement—the FSTMB—no longer had the leverage of the strike in the mines to force government concessions. The days of tin, as an exchange earning commodity for Bolivia, had come to a close; and, so too, had the economic leverage it provided the miners. That is, without tin, the miners were no longer miners. As desperate human beings needing to feed their families, they were inevitably forced to a position of "bargaining"—mostly through the use of group hunger strikes—for government sympathy.

Paz's "success" with the miners did not, of course, solve Bolivia's economic problems. Although the deregulation of prices on basic goods and the abolition of fixed exchange rates on Bolivian currency effected a need reduction in the rate of inflation, open employment in Bolivia for 1986 was estimated by the COB at nearly 30 percent. Some sources estimated the "real unemployment" rate for 1986 as high as 50 percent (Crabtree 1987, p. 20). This unemployment existed in the context of a country that had an overall infant mortality rate of 123 per 1000 live births (FIDA 1985, p. 1). The solution that Paz implemented with the "New Economic Policy" and increased taxation (including rural property tax) created and was bound to create further political problems into the late 1980s. From a "middle class" that could not pay for housing to a peasantry that was likely to resist the development of capitalist farming in the countryside, new political conflicts were bound to develop.

The problem of the development of capitalism in the countryside illustrates the structural or "modal" divergence in the Bolivian social formation. The insulation that silver and tin mining provided the noncapitalist mode of production that existed and continued to exist in the countryside had disappeared.[13] This meant that the brunt of capital accumulation was, by necessity, shifting to the peasantry. This economic requirement of the capitalist side was inevitably leading to new forms of articulation between the two sides. Conceivably, it could also lead to a new revolutionary conjuncture as the newly attempted forms of articulation at the economic and political level were resisted, with the ideology of the noncapitalist side (led by the *indígenista* movement) clashing with the ideology of the other.

The idea that a political clash between the two sides could actually cause a structural break (manifested in a revolution or rebellion) presupposes that the noncapitalist side of the social formation within Bolivia was such that it could move from a position of dependency on the capitalist side to one of domination (and seek political hegemony). The structural basis of such a possibility flows from an explanation of the recent structural history of the Bolivian social formation in the next chapter. The development of *katarista* (or any other *indígenismo*) hegemony would obviously not literally be the result of a resurgence of (or even a variant of) the Incan social formation. This, however, did not preclude the *katarista* movement from using an ideology that, in an original sense of a "revolutionary" appeal, made a case for change based upon perceptions of a given past reality. Granted that the *katarista* movement stood for something new on the Bolivian political scene, the next chapter, in one sense, may be seen as an attempt to give a structural underpinning to the politics of the *katarista* movement. At another level, the next chapter builds upon the information contained in this chapter to give a structural explanation for the politics of Bolivia, including the phenomenon of the *katarista* movement itself.

NOTES

1. Here, the term is used in something of the same way as Poulantzas (i.e., to distinguish a class that is distinct from the traditional Marxian notion of "petty bourgeoisie"). It should be noted, however, that this new petty bourgeoisie—not the result of the social process of monopoly capitalism—was not, strictly speaking, the new petty bourgeoisie described by Poulantzas. Nonetheless this term seems more accurate than simply calling it a "middle class" or "middle classes." It, like the new petty bourgeoisie of a monopoly capitalist formation, performed supervisorial and ideological roles that defined its place in the export-dominated economy of the capitalist mode of production of the late 1800s and early 1900s.

2. For a detailed account of the politics of the period from the turn of the twentieth century to the 1952 revolution, see Klein (1969).

3. The same source places the percentage of GDP of the primary sector—agriculture, mining, and petroleum—at 48.5; the tertiary sector encompassed 37.5 percent.

4. A common perception of the time was that the oligarchy had betrayed Bolivia to

Chile during the War of the Pacific in the 1870s, in which Bolivia lost its coastal territory.

5. *"Rosca"* was the Bolivian term for the prerevolution ruling class.

6. According to Andrew Pearse (1972), at the time of the revolution two thirds of the peasantry lived and worked within the hacienda system.

7. Among those elected were Victor Paz Estenssoro, Augusto Céspeds, and Walter Guevara Arze, all of whom later played major roles in the National Revolution.

8. The subject of minifundisimo and peasant ideology is discussed in the next chapter.

9. For example, Gulf oil's holdings were nationalized in the late 1960s by a nationalist faction of the military.

10. For the history of recurrent *indígenismo* see Albó & Barnadas 1985. For an excellent history of the modern *indígenismo, katarismo,* and for biographies of its principal leaders, see Hurtado (1986). Another useful source on *katarismo* and the development of the CSUTCB is Rivera 1984 *Oprimidos pero no vencidos.* One of the ideas that Rivera makes use of is that of the "collective memory" to explain the recurring and "undefeated" phenomenon of *indígenismo.* Rivera's 1984 book also contains the *tesis politica—1983* of the CSUTCB.

11. Notably, Reinaga is the exception in using the word *indio* instead of *campesino* or *indígena* in an intentional attempt to resurrect usage of the word. He did this to counter what he argued was a plan to smother the heritage of the *indio* on the part of the MNR through its replacement of *indio* with the racially neutral term of *campesino.*

12. On a personal note, I was living in the city of Santa Cruz during the Natusch coup and was thus, with my colleagues at the California Language Institute, somewhat anxiously compelled to follow the local military broadcasts, shortwave broadcasts, and daily rumors for information regarding the outcome of the standoff. After the resolution of the coup, the newspapers reported that fighting between the forces loyal to Natusch and those of the government had only been averted by the heavy rains that had made landing troop planes from the highlands impossible.

13. One possible replacement as the insulating factor was the foreign exchange earnings brought by the cocaine trade. Profits from this trade, however, were not being reinvested in Bolivia (see Doria 1986).

Chapter 5
Structural Results of Agrarian Reform

The fundamental proposition in this chapter is that events of 1952 and 1953 in Bolivia reflected a capitalist revolution of the urban sector that failed to extend to the indigenous zones of the countryside. Rather, events in those zones reflected a dynamic of a dominated noncapitalist mode of production, which, in effect, was politically and ideologically disjointed from the new ruling class produced within the capitalist mode of production of the urban mining sector. The social relations of production affecting the indigenous population were decisively changed in the events of 1952 and 1953; the hacienda system was destroyed. However, neither the indigenous *campesinado* political leadership in the countryside nor the MNR leadership of the urban, capitalist sector pushed for (or were compelled by economic forces to bring) capitalist farming to the indigenous zones of the *campo* at the time of the "National Revolution." This chapter is most specifically concerned with describing the type and level of economic articulation that began after the 1953 reform. The primary point is that the forms of economic articulation—market and labor migration—did not induce a change in the indigenous social relations of production. This, in turn, bears upon the continuing viability of the ideology, reflected in those social relations, that makes the indigenous mode resilient to capitalist subsumption.

By the 1980s it had become apparent to the political leadership of the capitalist side that the expansion of capitalism into the indigenous areas of the *campo* had become a structural imperative necessitated by the decline in the profitability of the mining industry. However, as of the mid-1980s, capitalism did not appear able to succeed as a prevailing mode of production in the indigenous areas of the *campo*. The methodological implication of the issue here is that if the extension of capitalist relations of production had been successful in the *campo*, there would be little justification for looking at the peasantry as a mostly homogenous whole. Under conditions of capitalism in the countryside, we should find diversity and differentiation as former peasants and/or outsiders made the move to capitalist farming—expanding landholding, cultivating for the marketplace, hiring wage laborers. If capitalism had not taken root, then we could expect to find relative homogeneity and the use of noncapitalist or at least noncapitalist-oriented strategies for survival. This latter set of conditions seems to be the better description of the Bolivian countryside in indigenous areas of the altiplano and the valleys.

In these areas of the *campo,* the indigenous mode of production maintained a certain structural cohesion, even though the "original" indigenous mode of production was very much twisted to meet the economic needs of the capitalist system carried by the Spanish. The dominant class place of the Incan social formation was eliminated by the Spanish, and mediating links were established (e.g., the position occupied by the *kuraka* and *wamani*)[1] between the Spanish and the reconfigured indigenous mode of production.[2] This restructuring, created in the interaction with the Spanish, did not, however, eliminate the ideological element or the class places involved in the reproduction of ideology—an ideology consistent with the process of production (and reproduction) of the *ayllu.* Neither did it eliminate the economic element of the indigenous mode. Although *indígena* labor was appropriated for the mining of silver, this form of articulation did not create a dynamic leading to the end of the indigenous control of the factors of production in the *campo* or the social relations associated with that control. Later, in the republic period of 1825 to 1952, the expansion of the hacienda by the Bolivian propertied class did directly subsume *indígena* labor to the economic system of the capitalist side. However, this subsumption, to use the distinction raised by Marx in his essay the "Results of the Immediate Process of Production," was "formal subsumption." That is, although *indígena* labor was forced to increase absolute surplus value and sacrifice that value to the hacendado, his or her own form of production was not substantially changed; it still remained in 1953 when the politically coerced creation of that surplus value was eliminated. As such, capitalism did not develop in the *indígena* zones of its own accord; the former labor and ideological processes were extant and created resistance to the development of capitalist processes of production.

In building and supporting this contention, I point to the historical trends of the Bolivian *indígena,* and to the cultural traditions that arose from the context of the cooperative labor relationships of the *comunidad.*[3] To preempt a justified critique of a similar argument, I am not arguing that the *indígena* is somehow "stupid," lazy, or economically "irrational" as some observers as late as the 1960s explained the noncapitalist tendencies of the *campesino.* Rather, I maintain that the *indígenas* of Bolivia share a particular history that is not conducive to capital accumulation by this group of people. Thus where these people remained—and remained in control of their own tools of production—they remained noncapitalist. This is not to argue that their condition was static or that they were not involved in their historic development. Rather, the argument here is that the logic of that mode of production that explains the situation of the Bolivian *indígena* precludes capitalist development from within and creates resistance to capitalist intrusion from without.

Certainly such a statement could have been made of many groups throughout the world as they faced capitalist domination and subsumption. The usual assumption is that such peoples are eventually displaced or transformed by capitalism. In the Bolivian case, however, the *indígena* remained in control of the factors of production in his or her own geographical zones and maintained the political will (driven by the ideological element) to continue that control.[4]

ARTICULATION AND DISARTICULATION

The pre-1953 hacienda system of labor extraction from the indigenous population did not eliminate the noncapitalist relations of production practiced by the *colonos*. Instead, the hacendados made use of indigenous notions (and previous European notions) to politically impose a process of tight articulation that effectively maintained noncapitalist relations of production. Bolivian scholar Antonio Rojas made this point in a 1980 *Latin American Perspectives* article:

> The articulation of the smallholding system with the economy of the hacienda tended to reproduce the relations of production which tied the tenant worker to his means of production because this assured the generation of agrarian rent through the legal appropriation of the land by the hacendado. But the nature of this unit of exploitation controlled by the landowner did not significantly modify the social and material conditions. (1980, p. 68).

The argument regarding the nature of the subsumption of the indigenous labor to a "capitalist" mode during the period from the arrival of the Spanish to the 1953 land reform is drawn out in Chapter 3, where I contend that the hacienda's use of *indígena* labor should be seen as "formal subsumption" (i.e., the taking of a labor process as it is found and extracting labor surplus to the benefit of capital accumulation) to a capitalist mode of production. Following the 1953 reform, the *indígena* laborer was disattached from any process of labor relating to the capitalist mode of production as long as he or she physically stayed in the *indígena* zone. Of course, many did not. Many crossed over to the urban sector to sell labor in the "particular" capitalist mode of production—as permanent migrants and as seasonal migrants to capitalist agricultural zones.

The immediate and most dramatic impact of the 1953 agrarian reform was the legal ending of the tight articulation process of the hacienda. That is, the immediate structural result of that change was the separation of the two modes at the economic level. This separation was nearly complete in terms of labor and, as seen in the shortages of food for the markets in the cities, in commodities. The immediate postreform shortage of food in the cities was seen by many as evidence of the inefficiency of the new form of production in the *campo*. However, the better analysis of that situation is that *campesinos* were suddenly free to increase their portion of the same total product for their own consumption (Albó 1983, p. 35).

This sudden appearance of "free time" was exactly what we would expect as the laborer left a process of labor extraction characterized by what Marx labeled the "formal subsumption" of a noncapitalist labor process to a particular capitalist mode of production. Marx made the point in his essay, "Results of the Immediate Process of Production," that

> capital subsumes the labor process as it finds it, that is to say, it takes over an existing labor process, developed by different and more archaic modes of production. . . . For example, handicraft, a mode of agriculture corresponding to a small, independent peasant economy. . . . The work may become more intensive, its duration may be extended, it may become more continuous or orderly under the eye of the interested capitalist, but in themselves these changes do not affect the character of the actual labor process, the actual mode of working" (1977, p. 1021).

In terms of structure, food redistribution was an effect of the immediate disarticulation and readjustment of the two modes. The immediate food shortage in the cities was alleviated as *campesinos* set aside more product for market.[5] Structurally, the two temporarily disjointed modes of production relinked at the economic level via food commodities that, following a short period of adjustment, transited the figurative gap of economically loosely articulated modes of production.

It has been pointed out by many observers of the market situation that the *campesinado* was unable to assure a price for any crop that he or she directed for the marketplace that was sufficient for covering the cost of producing that crop (including, of course, the opportunity cost of not growing produce for his or her family's own consumption). That is, the capitalist farmers of the eastern regions of Bolivia could, through mechanization and government subsidy, lower the price of the same (or substitute) *campesinado* products. The *campesinado*, however, given the insecurities already existing in the form of natural disaster that the peasant must face, can be viewed in purely economic terms as acting "rationally" to avoid the additional insecurity of price fluctuations in the marketplace.

Nonetheless, the *campesinado* participated in markets to the extent that excess production was available for the marketplace. The extent of actual market participation by the *campesinado* varied between regions. The Quechuas of the Cochabamba Valley tended to be more involved in the marketplace than the Aymaras of the altiplano. In any case, this market participation did not indicate a capitalist production process. To the extent that market participation did occur, it can be held that the income derived (at this point of articulation between the two modes) benefited the reproduction of the indigenous mode of production, possibly more so than it benefited the capitalist mode of production with a source of relatively high-cost food. Furthermore, to the extent that the capitalist side attempted to avoid paying the full cost (in terms of labor value), there was additional "rational" disincentive for the peasant to consider devoting more labor time to production for market.

Another area of re-articulation between the two modes of production occurred at the level of labor as *campesinos*, making use of their "free time," transited this figurative gap between modes to sell their labor power in the cities (where they might then choose to reside permanently) or in the capitalist sectors of agriculture (either permanently or seasonally). As reported by Antonio Rojas, one former peasant expressed the subjective side of this condition of release from the legal bonds of the hacienda as being "as if we had been given a permit of circulation, freedom to go wherever we wished" (1980, p. 82).[6] The structural implication of this movement was that the two modes relinked at the economic level via labor migration (as well as in circulation of agricultural products) from the indigenous zones of the countryside in the form of loose articulation as opposed to the tight articulation of the hacienda arrangement of articulation. That is, workers crossed from the *indígena* mode of production to the capitalist mode in the form of permanent and seasonal migration to the cities and capitalist rural areas. Whereas the labor that permanently migrated to the urban centers would seem to represent clear concessions to capitalist development,[7] the seasonal migration (mostly to the zones of capitalist agriculture in northern Argentina and, somewhat later, to the Santa Cruz or Oriente region of Bolivia) structurally represented a pattern of circulation across the gap between modes and which permitted, or was a causal component of, the overall persistence of the *indígena* mode of production.

ARTICULATION: SEASONAL MIGRATION TO ZONES OF CAPITALIST PRODUCTION

To understand the motivation for seasonal and permanent migration (of all sorts) of at least the majority of those migrants who originated in the *campo,* it is probably enough to point to the data on the physical conditions of reproduction in the countryside. Conditions in the countryside were such that the *campesinado* as a whole was not able to reproduce itself without relying upon the capitalist side. This is not to say that *indígena* agriculture was in any way inevitably bound to be replaced by the capitalist side of the social formation. Simply put, the peasant economy was not self-contained or capable of reproducing itself on an extended scale completely through self-sufficient agriculture. According to the World Bank the national average daily consumption of calories was 2,158 for 1982. That number of calories falls 10 percent short of the amount needed to satisfy nutritional requirements as estimated by the United Nations Food and Agriculture Organization [cited in *Fundo Internacional de Desarrollo Agrícola* (FIDA) 1986, p. 1]. It was this need that led members of households to seek income through permanent and seasonal migration to the capitalist agricultural regions of Bolivia (and northern Argentina).

This view of inadequate production for sustenance[8] in the campo as a, if not the, basic cause for most migration in Bolivia is supported by Javier Albó's study of those *campesinos* who had migrated to the city of La Paz.[9] Albó found, after discounting for ambiguous answers, that the lack of productive land was cited in 69.1 percent of concrete economic answers to his survey of the migrant population:

> In many cases the respondent declared that the migration was the result of a bad year or a bad harvest. The family found itself with insufficient resources to survive that year and so began the migratory process. Other common responses stated that there were too many brothers and the possessed land was not enough for everyone. . . (1981, pp. 63–64, my translation).

This point on the inadequate land availability is also demonstrated in the data from the 1976 agricultural census (reported in Riordan 1976). As alluded to in the quotation above, the phenomenon of *minifundisimo* meant that land worked by the parents was often not sufficient for division among the adult offspring. The size of a household's land correlated with principal activity of head-of-household and labor migration. First, the largest percentage of heads of "agricultural households" whose principal occupation was not in agriculture was highest among the group that owned less than 1 hectare. Thirteen percent of the heads of those households were primarily occupied outside agriculture. That this off-farm search for income must have been related to a search for subsistence emerges from the data in the category of 1 to 2 hectares of land in which the percentage of non-agricultural jobs drops to 6 percent; in all categories up to 20 hectares the same figure is 4 percent. That is, the hypothesis here is that those households with enough land for self-sufficiency were less likely to have engaged in a search for "extra income" from sources other than their own farm.[10] [The same figure for the category of 20 hectares or more is 6 percent (see Table 2.7 in Riordan 1983, p. 29).] Second, the greatest number and percentage of households with member(s) engaged in seasonal or permanent migration was among the less-than-one hectare group with 19,238 household affected by seasonal migration of a total of 58,224 households so affected, and 9,160 affected by permanent migration of a total of 22,601 so affected (Table 2.9 in Riordan 1983, p. 32). It should also be noted here that the category of less-than-one hectare (on this nationwide agricultural census) was also the category greatest occupied (on a per hectare basis) with a total of 108,866 out of a total number of 383,597 farms (or 28.4 percent) (Table 2.7 in Riordan 1983, p. 29). That is, small farms (and their economic consequences) were prevalent.

The major destination for seasonal migration within Bolivia was the capitalist agricultural sector of the department of Santa Cruz. The eastern region of Bolivia developed capitalist sugar and rice farming after the completion of a semi-paved road to Cochabamba in the early 1960s and the completion of rail links to Argentina and Brazil. The development of large farms and infrastructure for storage and processing was especially aided during the Banzer regime of the 1970s. However, state policies that led to the expansion of only a few crops—sugar cane, rice, and cotton—resulted in the agricultural production of the region becoming dependent on the ability to export and the world-market prices of those crops. Whereas from 1964 to 1975 land under cultivation for these crops grew at an annual rate of 9.3 percent, overproduction and low world market prices in the late 1970s forced a reduction of cultivated land in sugar cane, cotton, and rice of -4.3 percent annually between 1975 and 1980 [although the growth in the rate of production remained positive at between 4.7 percent and 2.5 percent (Vilar 1981, p. 15)]. This overproduction led to some diversification into new crops such as soy beans and sorghum. It also led to the production of more traditional crops such as corn and peanuts for the production of vegetable oils. This meant that the proportion of the three main crops diminished during the last half of the 1970s from 58 percent of total cultivated land to 38 percent in 1980 (Vilar 1981, p. 16).

This change in crop production was also reflected in the demand for labor.

Between 1975 and 1980 the percentage of labor involved in the production of the three predominant crops declined from 66 percent to 52 percent. Perhaps more significantly that same five-year period revealed a growing tendency toward mechanization at the production sites and a consequent need for a relatively smaller, but technically experienced, year-found labor force. Concurrent with the mechanization the average agricultural per unit demand for labor decreased from 72.9 laborer days/hectare in 1975 to 59.2 laborer days/hectare in 1980. However, because mechanization had not occurred in the harvesting phase, there was a relative increase in demand for seasonal workers—that is harvesters in the month of May (Vilar 1981, pp. 16–17).

Of those agricultural workers who held permanent employment, the majority had migrated to the area at least five years previous to the census (i.e., they were in the category *migrante antiguo*). The data from cotton and sugar cane show that 52.7 percent of the permanent labor force was *migrante antiguo* in cotton and 70.3 percent in sugar cane. Adding to this pattern of stability for permanent workers was that 21.7 percent of the permanent force in cotton was originally from the zone of the farm (i.e., had never migrated). (This figure was only 8.2 percent for sugar cane.) Also, of the remaining percentile, 20.1 percent of permanent workers in cotton who were reported as recent migrants were from the same department as the farm was located (i.e., Santa Cruz). Only 5.5 percent of the permanent workers in cotton were recent migrants from other departments. The respective figures for those in sugar cane production were 11.3 percent and 10.2 percent (Vilar 1981, p. 37). This pattern of employment of the permanent sector indicates that those peasants with insufficient land in the valleys or altiplano did not (or at least did not in the last five years previous to the 1978 study) make the transition to (or could not find) permanent jobs in the agricultural capitalist sector.

However, during the harvest seasons the labor force was flooded with seasonal migrants. Of the total labor force involved in harvesting cotton in the department of Santa Cruz, only 15 percent were not seasonal migrants, 8.1 percent were of the department of Santa Cruz, and 76.9 percent were migrants from other departments (Vilar 1981, p. 67). Of the sugar cane harvesters, 26.5 percent were not migrants, 14.7 percent were of the department of Santa Cruz, and 59.7 percent were migrants from other departments (Vilar 1981, p. 67). In a 1983 work on conditions faced by the *campesinado,* Albó estimated that each year 40,000 to 60,000 harvesters migrated to the department of Santa Cruz from indigenous zones (Albó 1983, p. 56).

Albó considered the possibility that the experience of these social agents who occupy two class places would facilitate the cultural integration of Bolivia, by exposing the workers of the interior to customs of the east and the Spanish language, and stimulate social change by introducing the worker to "scientific methods" of agriculture and oblige the worker to live for a time outside the traditional system of authority and organization. However, Albó found that the advantages to the workers were minimal in economic terms. Instead of hiring workers by contract (which would then make the wages and working conditions determined by law) they sought "voluntary" laborers (i.e., those not offered a contract to sign and thus not protected by the labor law). Thus, these workers who for the most part lived in unhealthful conditions had very little money or positive experience with which to return to the indigenous zones.

These low wages that Albó considered the reason for the decline in 1977 of a number of seasonal migrants (at the cost of sugar cane going unharvested), and the move to mechanization indicated the relationship of "superexploitation" between the workers from the indigenous zones and the capitalist agriculturalists of Santa Cruz. That is, with credit made available by favorable government (especially Banzer) policies, the capitalist farmers were able to mechanize and thus reduce the need for year-round labor (for which full reproduction cost would need to be paid).

The farmers' unwillingness to provide wages high enough to attract enough laborers to the sugar cane fields indicated their propensity to reduce wage costs to an absolute minimum, which of course was "rational." Their ability to pay laborers at a level beneath that necessary to attract sufficient labor to complete the harvest was also rational because the expansion of planting had been made possible with subsidies from the Bolivian government even when the world price of sugar did not justify the expansion of production (see Riester 1975). (That is, the price at market did not justify the cost of higher wages.)

On balance, then, seasonal migration to the capitalist zones of agriculture in the east was a point of economic articulation between the capitalist and indigenous modes of production. However, the capitalist farmers had demonstrated their propensity to mechanize and use the labor pool at harvest only to the extent warranted by the market price. The effects of these trends were that there was only a small amount of labor "capture" in this area of capitalist production, and the experience of the seasonal migrant worker was not conducive to the kind of technical education and cultural intermixing that observers might have expected.

Seasonal workers remained reliant upon their original communities. And, to the extent that their wages added to their income, seasonal migration contributed to the endurance of the indigenous mode of production as its members were able to infuse income obtained from the capitalist side. The economic effect on the indigenous mode of production of seasonal migration was similar to the effect obtained from income derived from the marketing of excess products in the capitalist side. As well, there was the same lack of control over, and relative disadvantage in, the marketplace—whether of indigenous produce or indigenous labor.

DISARTICULATION: BASIS OF IDEOLOGICAL DIVISION OF MODES OF PRODUCTION

As indicated by the available quantitative data, one of the most striking characteristics of the total Bolivian population and work force was its relatively high percentage of rural population. Much of the permanent migration that had taken place in Bolivia since the Reform was rural-rural. At least partially this rural-rural migration pattern may account for the fact that Bolivia was a close second to Paraguay in percentage figures on least amount of urbanization of the Latin American countries. In 1960, 32.1 percent of the Bolivian population lived in cities of more than 2,000 inhabitants. This figure compares to 31.0 percent for Paraguay in that year. By 1970 the Bolivian figure for urbanization had moved only to 39.8 percent whereas the figure for Paraguay had moved to 36.0 percent. In 1980 the (estimated) percentage for Bolivian urbanization was 48.7 percent and 43.2 percent for Paraguay (Cuadro III.2 in Casanovas 1981, 38). In terms of occupation, whereas 72.1 percent of the economically active population was involved in agriculture in 1950, this figure had declined to the still quite high percentage of 46.4 percent for the 1976 census.[11] A World Bank study calculated the percentage of total Bolivian population involved in agriculture to be at 55 percent (using a total population figure of 5.7 million) (1984, p. 2).

The data describing the nature of the Bolivian agriculturalist indicate that the category of "small agriculturalist" was the largest category within the Bolivian population. Of the total estimated population for 1985, 42.2 percent were placed in the category of *pequeños agricultores* (small farmer—indicating peasant farmer) and 4.9 percent were placed in the category of *asalariados agrícolas*. This 4.9 percent for 1985 was nearly constant with the 1976 figure of 5.0 percent of salaried agricultural workers. The percentage of "peasant farmers" was placed at 47 percent in 1976 (i.e., with a drop of 4.8 percent in the 1985 data). In the same study the breakdown of "peasant farmers" as a percentage of total rural population was 73.8 percent, with the highest regional figure being in the valleys with a figure of 79.4 percent and 76.9 percent in the altiplano and a relatively low 50 percent in the "plains"—Santa Cruz region. Whereas the same breakdown for salaried or wage workers indicated only 7.2 percent of the total rural population worked for wages, 28.1 percent of the rural population in the plains were in this category; 3.9 percent of the rural population were salaried workers in the valleys, and only 1.2 percent of the rural population were salaried workers in the altiplano. It is notable that the regional breakdown of the salaried agricultural workers indicates that from 1976 to 1985 the percent of salaried agricultural workers of the total population remained constant except for a slight *decrease* in the plains from 3.4 percent to 3.3 percent. There was also an increase from 5.8 percent to 6.5 percent of "small farmers" in the plains. Nonetheless, as indicated in the rural breakdown figures above, the *llanos* or plains of eastern Bolivia remained the area where the largest percentage of agricultural wage labor existed. This of course reflected its status as the area newly opened to capitalist exploitation "from above" following the Reform[12] [*Fundo Internacional de Desarrollo Agricola* (FIDA) 1985, p. 8].

This capitalist exploitation of the eastern zone of Bolivia is also reflected in the regional breakdown of average size of property holdings. Whereas in 1978 the average size of an *"exploitación"* in all of Bolivia was 5.4 hectares, the average size of a farm in the department of Santa Cruz was 19.4 hectares, and the average net income of the farm in Bolivian pesos was $b21,294; this compared to an average size of 3.2 hectares and a net average income of $b8,206[13] in the department of Cochabamba (Riordan 1983, p. 38).

A 1984 World Bank report on Bolivia stated the following case regarding the development of capitalism in the *campo*:

> Most Bolivian farmers live in a subsistence economy. Their main objective is to reach a level of production that assures survival while minimizing risks. The farmer's economic activities are organized to this end, and are the outcome of behavior patterns, production techniques, and social conventions that have been tested and adjusted over centuries. . . . To adopt modern techniques would expose him to an unacceptable level of risk . . . (1984, p. 2).

The *campesinado* of Bolivia was not capitalist and not likely to become so.

Furthermore, this persistence of the *indígena* mode of production is indicated by the separation and continuation of the *indígena* languages. (Indeed this separation of *indígena* from *blanco* may be seen in Bolivian use of the word *"campesino,"* which indicates not a peasant but an indigenous person.) But to further substantiate the division that exists in Bolivian society one can point to the split that exists in language, which corresponds to the division between capitalist and *indígena* mode of production. In 1950 one million Bolivians spoke only Quechua, and 664,000 Bolivians spoke only Aymara. As late as 1976 over one fifth of the population spoke no Spanish at all. In rural areas the

1976 census data indicate that 17.1 percent of the males and 27.4 percent of the females spoke only Quechua; 8.2 percent of the males and 15.9 percent of the females spoke only Aymara (Albó, "Lengua y sociedad en Bolivia 1976," Instituto Nacional Estatistica 1980). The relationship of principal use of *indígena* language to small, subsistence farming is confirmed by data from the 1976 agricultural census, which show that the use of Spanish as the principal language of the agricultural household increased with the size of the *"exploitación."* Only 12 percent of the agricultural households of less than 1 hectare used Spanish as the primary language. On the other hand, 40 percent of the households with 20 hectares or more used Spanish as the primary language (Riordan 1978, p. 28).

A common response in Bolivia was that these figures must be declining as more Quechua and Aymara children go through the national system of Spanish-language education and concomitantly are "socialized" into the Bolivian nation. However, this argument is contradicted in a study by Eloy Anello for USAID in the mid-1970s, which found that the typical rural school principal assumed that classes conducted in Spanish would automatically result in non-Spanish-speaking students learning Spanish. The high dropout rate in the primary grades was one painful indication that the process did not work.[14] Furthermore, little resource was being used to correct the situation in the 1980s.[15] This point is also supported by the available data regarding an attendance rate of school-age children of 35.7 percent in the rural areas of Bolivia compared to a rate of 99.82 percent for the urban areas of Bolivia (CEDOIN, "La educación en la crisis y la crisis de la educación," *Informe Especial* 1987, p. 13).[16]

Further, there is a population of *indígena* that resides in the comunidades—zones of *indígena* social and production units that never came under the control of the hacienda system.[17] Further, there was a group composed of merchants or *comerciales*. As indicated by the expansion from 8.2 percent of the economically active population in 1950 to 18.9 percent in 1976, the category of *servicios, comerciales, sociales y personales* was swelled by the labor-freeing effects of the agrarian reform.

Technically, then, it would seem that the *indígena* (as a mass) could be divided on the basis of economic organization and distinctive relations to the capitalist mode of production into at least six groups. First, there were indigenous populations able to exist and reproduce themselves and their social relations of production within their *comunidades* of indigenous origin. Second, a closely related group was the smallholding peasantry also in control of its own tools of production and able to reproduce its own minimum conditions of existence including their social relations of production in market articulation with the capitalist mode of production. Third, there were permanent rural wage workers in the capitalist side. Fourth, there were individuals of the first and second groups who seasonally migrated into capitalist rural wage conditions. Fifth, there were urban *indígenas* who lived and reproduced as (subemployed) workers within if not of the capitalist side. Sixth, there were *indígenas* who engaged in merchant activity. The question then becomes one of what, if any, are the class distinctions to be made here? This in turn leads to the question of ideology—particularly in this situation in which the social formation contains two clearly distinct modes of production and two "dominant" modalwide ideologies.

CONCLUSION

The *indígena* mode of production maintained its own "class place" of direct producer, which was never "really" subsumed (as in "real" versus "formal subsumption") by the foreign capitalist mode. This meant that after the land reform in 1953 the indigenous mode of production was not, as some might suppose, a remnant of a dead historical era. Rather, the *indígenas* of these areas lived in a manner consistent with the social relations that are best explained by reference to the concept of a noncapitalist mode of production. These social relations were manifested in a form of social cooperation that was qualitatively distinct from the form of social cooperation characteristic of a capitalist mode of production.

I refer to this noncapitalist mode of production that is useful in explaining the Bolivian social formation as an *"indígena* (or indigenous) mode of production." This *indígena* mode of production may be understood in the context of the Bolivian social formation through social relationships that were based upon intragroup cooperation (or reciprocity) in the use of labor, and in the distribution of surplus among members through such noncapitalist mechanisms as religious ceremonies. These noncapitalist social relationships were driven and perpetuated by ideological factors (e.g., indigenous religion). This religious element also significantly affected the maintenance of a noncapitalist mode of production in other ways. For example, the sacred consideration of the land (the "Pachamama" or earth mother) meant that few *indígenas* were willing to either sell their land or put it at risk as collateral to obtain more land, better seed, or equipment. Also, as in the case of peasants universally, the Bolivian *campesinos* were distinguished from laborers in a capitalist mode of production by the self-ownership and control of the tools of production in their zones of the countryside.

The form of cooperation and social relations within the social group of the indigenous mode is of a different nature, not simply of a different degree, than those social relations found in a capitalist process of production. That is, cooperation among the *indígenas* was connected to a pattern of thought, or ideology, that did not require individual action to be determined by the pursuit of self-interest. This indigenous mode of production was an economic, political, and ideological structural process that had existed historically as the prevailing mode in a previous social formation (i.e., Incan society). Speaking of the period since the revolution and agrarian reform, the indigenous mode of production, as part of the "Bolivian social formation," continued to exist (i.e., to have theoretical validity) as it explained or accounted for the dynamics of the "peasant" or *indígena* attribute of the social formation.

The next chapter carries forward an analysis of the ideological element as it is reflected in indigenous social relations. In doing this, it examines the technical distinctions drawn above among the indigenous population and argues that the evidence supports the validity of a rather large single classification of the indigenous side. A key question remains about the position of the intermediary class. From which side does its ideological determination come? That is, was this historically key class determined by its political authority as granted by the capitalist side or was its political authority granted through the ideological element of the indigenous side? As discussed in Chapter 4, the organization that replaced the government sponsored peasant union and gained its authority based upon appeal to the ideology of the indigenous side was the Confederación Sindical Unica Trabajadores Campesinado de Bolivia (CSUTCB).

From its inception the CSUTCB relied on the notion of a separate ideology as much as, or probably more than, the notion of an exploited class or classes as the basis for opposing the dominant capitalist economy. It is the ideology of *indígenismo* or *katarismo* upon which the CSUTCB based much of its endeavor for social change. In Chapter 2, the Poulantzian conception of mode of production was introduced as the basic concept for application to the Bolivian situation largely because of its explicit use of ideology in the mode of production scheme and class analysis. In the following chapter, I apply that analysis—particularly the use of political and ideological criteria in the determination of class place— to the Bolivian social formation of the mid-1980s.

NOTES

1. See Taussig on role of the *"wamani"* (1980, p. 196).
2. This process of disruption and response is covered in some detail in Chapter 3.
3. The history of the *indígena* mode of production is covered in Chapter 3.
4. As discussed in Chapter 2, theoretical emphasis on the ideological element of a mode of production is a feature derived from Poulantzas' analysis of the mode of pro-

duction as continuing three essential processes—each of which may determine the whole.

5. The nature of the markets themselves changed as *transportistas* (many of whom were recently "freed" labor) began operations into more remote areas, which in turn created more remote, smaller markets that fed into the larger markets of the cities.

6. In the article cited here, Rojas seems to beg the question by stating that this freed labor made the conditions for capital continually better. Whereas it is certainly true that a cheap labor supply improves necessary conditions for capitalist development it does not improve or lead to sufficient conditions for capitalist development. In Bolivia, much of the freed labor went into merchant capital activity (associated with rural and urban areas, and which, some have argued, may be a drag on capitalist development). In any case, Rojas completes his conclusion to his article by listing the impact of this freed labor in terms of "the reduction of its [labor's] value as a commodity and the super-exploitation which it produces to facilitate a low organic composition of capital; the creation of an enormous labor mass whose agricultural production is integrated into the terms of intersectoral exchange at a deficit; and the expansion of the internal market for industry. In this fashion, the small " 'self-sufficient' domestic unit of production is unprotected against the strong wind of the market economy." This last point of an unprotected domestic unit of production is also suspect as peasants were able to remain inward looking in terms of self-sufficient production (with the reproduction process supplemented when necessary by seasonal migration to capitalist zones of rural production in Argentina and the Santa Cruz region of Bolivia and/or family members who had entered the cities without necessarily entering the capitalist mode of production directly; this process is discussed below). It is true that the more market-oriented strategies of the Quechaus in the Cochabamba Valleys were affected by price fluctuations they could not control. However, in the case of the more "inward-oriented" Aymaras and isolated Quechuas the problem was one of inability to extend reproduction of their relations of production due to such factors as land availability.

7. The position of the CSUTCB (in their political statement) and of Rivera (who develops the notion of "collective memory" to help explain the survival of an *indígena* ideology among the *indios* and/or *cholos* of the cities) is that the *indígena* who has migrated to the city has not been captured by the capitalist side. Albó's (*Chukiyawu* series) work is relevant on this point as well.

8. This argument regarding basic motivation for emigration from one rural area to the city or to another rural area can be found in the writings of many Bolivian authors on the subject. Some, for example Roberto Vilar, contend that while migration is indeed for the purpose of completing the reproduction process of the peasantry (or *"semi-proletariado"*—reflecting the process of seasonal migration), it was induced by the need for money to purchase the commercial goods that have become a part (i.e., a new necessity of reproduction) for this new class. This argument lays the stress for the motivation of migrants on the desires of *compesinos* for commercial items. This argument seems to be forcing the idea that commercial or merchant capital is the main reason for the breakdown of traditional social formation—including European feudalism—onto the Bolivian situation. It is somewhat suspect, I think, in that the argument presumes that commercial goods are able to insinuate themselves directly into the reproduction process of a traditional economy. And, as such, people would leave their land (which would be sufficient for survival) in order to obtain what would have to be a "luxury" good—not

food. I agree with the Albó argument—which he backs with survey data—that the majority of migration occurred because peasant-held land was inadequate to the task of supporting the *expansion* of reproduction of the peasanty.

9. As for migration to urban areas, I contend below (in discussing ideology and links to the *comunidades*) that this does not automatically represent insertion of the migrant into the capitalist mode of production. It does change the class place of the migrant. But that class place can be within the indigenous mode of production.

10. I am assuming that few individuals who have jobs outside of agriculture seek to supplement their principal activity by obtaining a small farm.

11. The area of largest percentage increase was in the category of *"servicios, comerciales, sociales y personales,"* which went from 8.2 percent in 1950 to 18.9 percent of the economically active population in 1976 (Cuadro V.7 in Casanovas 1981, p. 105).

12. The Santa Cruz and Beni region of Bolivia were regions in which there was not an indigenous population previously in control of the land as farmers. Consequently, the capitalist development of the eastern zones of Bolivia fits the main thesis of this chapter that capitalism had not extended to those regions where the *indígena* remained in control of the land.

13. I do not know what the exchange rate with the U.S. dollar was at that time; these figures are intended only to indicate relative income.

14. Information regarding Anello's conclusion reported here was obtained in conversation with Anello in August, 1985.

15. During my 1986 stay in Bolivia, public school teachers were making the equivalent of $15 a month. (After striking and negotiations, the salary was doubled.) In an economy where the OAS saw fit to provide "subsistence" stipends of the equivalent of $600 per month for one researcher, one is readily able to understand the plight of the public school teacher, many of whom in the 1980s left public teaching for jobs in the informal economy.

16. The author of the CEDOIN special report points to the fact that "Bolivia is not very strong in statistics," and demonstrates in this case why the 99.82% figure for urban areas is unrealistically high. It should be noted that as a whole the statistics generated by INE have been widely criticized as inaccurate.

17. The history of these *comunidades* and their relationship to the Spanish and Republican side are examined in Chapter 3.

Chapter 6

Mode of Production, Class, and Dominant Ideology of the *Campesinado*

This chapter argues that despite the technical distinctions of economic activity presented in the preceding chapter, the *campesinado* can be viewed as a single grouping, marked by a distinctive ideology, within a noncapitalist mode of production. Within that modal grouping, there are class distinctions that result mostly from its articulation with the capitalist mode of production. The primary class distinction is between those social agents who are direct producers, marked by noncapitalist ideology, and those social agents who fill a class category that is the political articulation between the two modes of production. That is, whereas merchants fill an economic determined category that is the economic articulation of the two modes of production, political agents fill places that are the political articulation between the two modes. Before getting at this point, however, this chapter presents the analysis of class and Bolivian society contained in the political documents of the CSUTCB. While showing the problems resulting from the ethnic-based analysis, this chapter attempts a structural understanding of the class and modal divisions within the Bolivian population. The end argument is that the CSUTCB may be right about class unity of the *campesinado* qua indigenous population, but for the wrong reasons.

This chapter uses the ideological feature of the indigenous mode of production, as it is expressed in relations of production, to demonstrate the historical continuation and increased significance of the intermodal articulation at the political level in the form of an intermediary class. That is, there is a structural basis for the political unity among most of the indigenous population and simultaneously a structural basis (or means of understanding) the potential for disarticulation as well as co-optation at the political level.

The basic assertion regarding the Bolivian case is that the *indígena* side of the social formation carried its own dominant ideology within its relations of production and reflected in its own ideological apparatuses (i.e., within its own "civil society") of religion, political parties, and social movements. This ideology had remained (reproduced) in the process of social reproduction within the indigenous mode of production; and, with regional variation and modification in response to the mode's articulation at all levels with the capitalist mode, had remained intact historically from the arrival of the Spanish to the present. The evidence of this ideology can be found in the ideological practices that had survived and resisted European subsumption. Although the religious practices or rituals of the indigenous side were not the ideology itself, they were indications that a separate ideology had been maintained.

Michael Taussig notes that the indigenous population of the Andes continued to carry out their religious ceremonies even if under the cover of Catholicism:

> Despite four centuries of humiliation and vicious subjugation, preconquest institutions still flourish in the Andes. . . . In general terms preconquest institutions have survived because Indian communities managed to wall themselves off from intrusive cultural influences. But they have survived also because the force of cultural intrusion stimulated a culture of resistance . . . (1980, p. 159).

Silvia Rivera Cusicanqui developed the concept of "collective memory" to explain the continued and "reawakening" ideological opposition to capitalist (or *blanco*) domination (external to the immediate process of production). In an essay on the *katarista* movement,[1] Rivera identified two "messianic" elements as the nucleus of the *katarista* ideology, "that are crystallized in the cultural-political dimension of the movement":

> 1. *katarismo* [was] a synthesis between a perfect ethical order, manifested in the Incan moral code (*ama sua, ama llula, ama q'ella*) and the anticolonial struggle that acts to restore it. Here the central point is the perception of the continuation of colonial situation that justifies the watchwords [*consignas*] of reestablishment of the prehispanic order.
>
> 2. *katarismo* [was] consciousness of the return of the hero, multiplied by thousands [from the last words, according to oral tradition, of Tŭpac Katari before being executed by the Spanish]: I die today, but tomorrow I shall return as thousands of thousands. Here the central point is the perception of the political quality of numbers: the notion of the *majority* national ethnic group, associated to the notion of "waking" the "sleeping giant" (in *Bolvia, hoy* 1983, pp. 163–64; my translation).

In addition to this long "horizon" of cultural-political memory, Rivera distinguishes a shorter horizon or dimension of the *katarista* movement existing from the events and changes brought about by the 1952 revolution. This second dimension of memory, she argues, can be interpreted as a syndicalist dimension, which corresponded to the political participation of the *campesino* via the organization of *sindicatos*. The continuity of the indian identity and anticolonial struggle was tainted (*matizada*) by the rupture that signified the revolutionary situation of 1952 and the move of "indio" to "campesino." Rivera uses this notion to help explain the political divisions between the Aymaras of the altiplano and the Quechuas of the valleys:

> The synthesis between the long-term memory (anticolonial struggles and pre-Hispanic social order) and the short-term memory (revolutionary power of the peasant *sindicatos* and militia beginning in 1952) is in reality a dialectical and contradictory process, that was expressed around the middle of the 1970s in a primary regional differentiation within the *campesino* movement. The quechua campesinado of Cochabamba, that [had experienced] a process of *"mestizaje"* much more intense and prolonged [that the aymaras of the altiplano], was fully incorporated in the revolution of 1952, and constituted the center of the syndicalist para-state apparatus mounted by the MNR (1983, p. 164; my translation).

Rivera explains that this is the reason that the *campesinado* of the valleys did not develop autonomous political movements and remained linked to the *criollo* parties and to the military. The representation of their interests by these parties was made acceptable to the Quechua *campesinado* because of its self-perception as "citizens." Put in other terms, the "ideological state apparatus" succeeded, for a period, in the Cochabamba valleys.

In the case of the altiplano, the incorporation of the aymara *campesinado* in the state project of 1952 was imperfect:

> The collective memory of the 1952 revolution meant only a partial rupture with the past, confronting the continuation of the practices of discrimination and political servitude [*"pongueaje politico"*]. The indian identity was only tinted by the revolutionary action of 1952. . . . The *katarista* movement of the aymaran altiplano expressed [the contradictions] that evidenced the failure of the MNR's project of cultural homogenization (1983, p. 165).

The Aymaras, unlike the Quechuans, did not respond to the *criollo* political parties. The perception of continued colonization and the "long-term memory" predominated over the "short-term memory."

PROBLEM OF ETHNICITY AND CLASS

As discussed in Chapter 4, the CSUTCB evolved out of the *katarista* movement and was primarily concerned with building the basis for unity among the several different indigenous groups in Bolivia, including the *indios* (ethnically) who had entered the capitalist side of the social formation. The heart of the CSUTCB argument as contained in its 1983 political document was that the *indígena* in Bolivia (including those who had entered the capitalist side of the formation) was oppressed by the *blanco*. This oppression began with the invasion of the Spanish and the destruction of the Incan social formation. This Incan social formation was described or, rather, mythologized as a society that did "not know hunger, thievery or lies" (Rivera 1984, p. 189).

With the arrival of the Spanish, the *indígena* in Bolivia became a "second class," determined or demarcated by its common "oppression" by the *blanco* economic system. To maintain the logical basis for such a unity, the analysis of the CSUTCB could neither be strictly an ethnic analysis (i.e., promoting the unity of a particular group such as the Aymaras, though that may be historically accurate) nor could it use a traditional structural conception of class as that would divide rural landholders from urban workers. The result was that the CSUTCB argued for something in between: a class that is defined as a group that has a common oppressor. The 1983 document presented the argument that the "diverse peoples" of Bolivia were engaged in a common struggle against the Spanish and the dominant classes of the Republic who had converged the indigenous groups to a "second class":

> This also applies to many workers in the country and the cities who have lost . . . the roots of their own culture, but who are also victims of the *dominant colonial mentality.* **Because all of us are oppressed, we have a common cause of liberation** (in Rivera 1984, p. 188; my translation italicization for emphasis is mine; bold print for emphasis is original).

The authors of the document also contended that the *campesinado* (qua *indígena*) was not diminishing, and that it was not divided by internal class distinctions. In its analysis of the "social and economic structure" of Bolivia, the CSUTCB contended that the dominant mode of production was the "dependent capitalist mode of production with colonial characteristics," within which the *campesinos* were the primary or "essential" exploited group in Bolivia:

> It is as producers of food and cheap primary materials, or as providers of manual labor, that we have fed with our sweat the growth of the mines and cities and the enrichment of a minority of *exploiters* (in Rivera 1984, p. 189; my translation).

The authors of the document maintained that this "essential" characteristic of the *campesinado* to the dominant mode of production, and the fact of its numbers, meant that the *campesinado* was not a "marginal or decadent class."

The authors further argued that the *campesinado* should not be identified as a petty bourgeoisie simply because it held parcels of land; rather, their control of land was a control of their heritage and identity. Only secondarily was it their means of production. Furthermore, the authors contended that differences of "social and economic" standing were not barriers to unity:

> Whether as peons of the agri-businesses or as small producers in agriculture, cattle ranching, fishing, or forestry, we share the same suffering and discrimination. **Because we are all workers of the *campo*, we have a common cause of liberation** (1984, p. 189; my translation).

The first criticism that could be made of the argument is that the concept of class and exploitation was not clearly defined. As indicated in the quotation above, the oppressors are "exploiters." The "dependent capitalist mode of production" in Bolivia had exploited or used the "sweat and blood" of the *indígena* to build its "mines and cities." In effect, the document placed the "exploited" into the "dependent capitalist mode of production" as one class. This leads to the second criticism that this class is apparently only secondarily identified by its place in the production process. The CSUTCB document uses the *campesinado* (qua indigenous people) to provide a single category for the oppressed/exploited. As a whole, the analysis is a seemingly contradictory mix of ethnic category with class category.[2]

This mix of *indígenismo* and ideas of class exploitation is not unique to the CSUTCB. Ideas of *indígenismo* can be found in the work of the Peruvian writer José Carlos Mariátegui. According to Sheldon Liss, Mariátegui sought to restore the old Incan communal land patterns to alleviate land tenure problems and put power in the hands of the population. Like the CSUTCB, Mariátegui extolled the virtues of pre-Columbia life and values as a stimulus to revolution.

For Mariátegui, the Incan past represented characteristics that were complimentary to a socialist projection for the future (Liss 1984, pp. 135–36).

In Bolivia, Tristán Marof (or Gustavo Adolfo Navarro), founder of the Trotskyist Partido Obrero Revolucionario (POR) in 1934 and the Partido Socialista Obrero Boliviano (PSOB) in 1938, advocated violent revolution linked to the return to indigenous political and social traditions and to the return of land to the Indians. In his 1934 book, *La tragedia del altiplano*, he praised the greatness of the pre-Columbian civilizations, condemned the Spanish for degrading them, and noted that the Incas understood and could cope with the problems of their times. He also categorized the Incas as a communial society, not a classless state and he noted that the Incan government was autocratic (Liss 1984, pp. 183–84).

Generally speaking, as noted in Chapter 4, the nationalism that developed in Bolivia in response to the Chaco War—as indicated in the cited RADEPA document—incorporated the *indio* as the basis for a true Bolivian identity, and the liberalism of the MNR and other urban-based groups at least gave lip service to the idea of the greatness of the pre-Columbian indian past. However, the liberal revolution of 1952 and the consequent agrarian reform of 1953 did not, in fact, act upon the ideas of a return to the *ayllu* or community-based economic units in the *campo*. Also, as discussed in Chapter 4, neither did the 1952 revolution act to extend capitalist farming to the indigenous zones of the *campo*. The revolution in relations of production in the countryside (and relations of exchange to the urban side) remained "uncompleted." This completion or fulfillment of the indigenous promise became the task of the CSUTCB recognized as such in the 1983 Political Thesis:

> We are the inheritors of great civilizations. We are also inheritors of a permanent struggle against any kind of exploitation and pressure. We want to be free in a society without exploitation or oppression organized in a multi-ethnic State that develops our culture and authentic forms of self-government (in Rivera 1984, p. 187).

The *katarista* movement itself, from which the CSUTCB emerged, split into several political parties at least partially on the question of class versus indian nationalism. Whereas Fausto Reinaga's party, the Movimiento Indio Tupaj Katari (MITKA), was explicitly an *indio* (without class) party, the Movimiento Revolucionario Tupaj Katari (MRTK) did "not exclude but rather [gave] a certain priority to class analysis" (Albó 1987, p. 402).[3] From the perspective of the structuralist analysis I am presenting, this problem of class and ethnicity cannot be overstepped.

The key question is that of whether or not this group labeled *campesinos* by the CSUTCB can be or should be identified as a class. First, it should be clear that this use of the word *campesino* is in the sense of an indigenous person. As such, a *campesino* is not someone who necessarily engages in (or occupies) a "place" that is in a distinctive relationship to the means of production. The key element used to justify the concept of a "second class" as an encompassing category by the CSUTCB in its 1983 document is that of a common oppressor and a common interest in "liberation" from the oppressor. In fact, this implicit definition of "class" is similar to the one offered by E. P. Thompson in the *Making of the English Working Class:*

> Class happens when some men, as a result of common experiences (inherited or shared), feel and articulate the identity of their interests as between themselves, and as against other men whose interests are different from (and usually opposed to) theirs. . . . Class-consciousness is the way in which these experiences are handled in cultural terms: embodied in traditions, value-systems, ideas, and institutional forms (1966, pp. 9–10).

As well as the presence of the historical element of class used by Thompson, there is the notion of a common opponent—the capitalist ruling class. In the past, rebellious indian groups may not have recognized their commonality with all other indian groups, but isolated (and a few not so isolated) rebellions against the Spanish or the hacendado had marked the history of "blanco"—*indígena* relations qua economic and political relations of a particular context. The implicit point of the CSUTCB in the mid-1980s was that the common enemy of the *indígena* was the alien presence of capitalism; and, to fight it, the *indígena* must be united. To follow the point out, the basis of that unification was not a single ethnic identity (which had never existed) but rather the recognition that the *indígena* was an exploited/oppressed people. The obvious question then is does this mean that the concept of "oppressed" (or exploited) equals the concept of *indígena* for the makers of CSUTCB argument? That is, if one is oppressed in Bolivia is one then an *indígena*? Obviously, if the word *indígena* is to retain an ethnic connotation, the answer is no. It is on this point that the CSUTCB is most liable to the charge of racism. At the least, it is where the contradiction between a class designation and an ethnic designation is its most glaring.

The CSUTCB *indigenista* argument relied upon the fact that *indígenas* had not and did not as a rule enter the capitalist side of the social formation as dominators.[4] The CSUTCB strategy also relied upon the development of "consciousness" among the whole *campesinado* of its identity as *indígena* against *blanco,* which is also a notion found in the Thompson idea of "class." That is, that the group in question recognizes itself (i.e., "is present at its making") as a group with interests in opposition to those of another. It is this development (based in the dominant traditions of past social formations) in "cultural terms and values" that the CSUTCB (and the *katarista* movement) was promoting in the 1980s.

There are two major problems here. First, though the CSUTCB argument identifies or diagnoses the situation in Bolivia as a situation where the one social formation has been dominated by an invading capitalist social formation (and labels the capitalist as the "exploiters"), the analysis pulls short of an articulation of modes-of-production analysis. That is, it asserts that the one side (or rather "second class") is "oppressed" by the other; but, other than to place it within a "dependent capitalist mode of production," it fails to demonstrate how that "oppression" takes place. This means that even though the CSUTCB document speaks in terms of a "second class," its analysis leaves open the possibility that the CSUTCB is discussing the clash of "nations," not the clash (or response to exploitation) between classes or, for that matter, a relation of exploitation within the articulation of the one mode with the dominant mode.

This leads to the second major problem that despite claims to the contrary, the CSUTCB analysis risks being interpreted as meaning that the nature of the relation of exploitation that existed between the indigenous mode of production and the capitalist mode of production did not contain an economic element but was rather a problem of *blancos* (acting from motives of racism) prejudicing the condition of the *indígena.* That is, the exploitation of which the thesis speaks could be considered as being not a result of the process of production in Bolivia but of the ideological factor of racism.[5] The basis of this problem would seem to be the CSUTCB's theoretical insistence on the primacy of ethnicity even if only for the purpose of developing a "class consciousness." If the problem with capitalism in Bolivia were only that it is accompanied by attitudes of white racism, then the CSUTCB would only need to commit itself to a reform of Bolivian institutions (i.e., the removal of racism from the workplace and civil society). The problem of "oppression" could be solved by the mainstream (capitalist side) reformer who calls for the unification of the *indígena* into a single civil society with a capitalist production process. (Or, from the standpoint, of the "reformer," the production process and the class structure found in it would not be a relevant problem.) This effectual dropping of class analysis (which, as seen from the quotations above, was not apparently the intention of the CSUTCB) is the weakness of "class place" being confused with "class position" that Poulantzas in part directed his 1978 work against. That is, the methodological problem of an analysis that relies upon ethnic identification (and ideological factor external to the process of production) to assign class identification is that it fails to account for the structural basis of class.

Despite the ambiguity of class or ethnicity, the CSUTCB (as an organization based in *indígenismo*) raised ideology to a political level. That is, *indígenismo* was purposely used by the CSUTCB to unite otherwise disparate groups of people. If this had been a case of a political party formulating a tactic for the basis of a class alliance (class "position"), we might well suspect such a party of using an ideological mirage[6] to create the basis for temporary class alliances. However, as argued below, because this articulated ideology was based in the reproduction processes of a noncapitalist mode of production, we can explain the *katarista* movement in terms of the process of that reproduction.

CLASS PLACE OF DIRECT PRODUCER

From a typical structuralist point of view it is difficult to contend, as the CSUTCB document does, that the diverse classes (as defined by their relation to the means of production)[7] could be of one class. For example, how is it that a "peasant" (qua self-sufficient agriculturalist) could remain a peasant when he or she enters new relations of production as, say, a construction worker in a city? To explain this contention, I turn next to a discussion of the existing components of the *indígena* mode of production, class, and the effect of capitalist class place on those indigenous people who have crossed from the social relations of the *indígena* side to the capitalist side.

As discussed in Chapter 3, the Incan social formation contained three separate social classes: the ruling family, the priesthood and local leadership, and the direct producers. These social classes were defined according to economic, political, and ideological criteria. Since 1953, the class place of direct producer within the indigenous mode of production is occupied by the members of the remaining *comunidades,* the smallholding peasantry, and members of the pioneer communities (to the extent that they shared the values and economic relationships discussed below). Although there are several technical divisions that could be made, the three divisions among the indigenous population (of direct producers) that can be made on the basis of place within (or between) the two major modes of production are the small-holding peasantry, the seasonal migrant worker, and the permanent agricultural and urban worker in the capitalist mode of production. In the section below, I discuss each of these groups in terms of the degree of noncapitalist ideology that reflected their economic relations.

Of these categories, the largest is that of the small-holding (indigenous) agriculturalist who does not seasonally migrate. In discussing the small-holding peasant on the altiplano and in the valleys, one must be aware of the economic practices and influence of the Incan *ayllu* or, what has become known in Bolivia as, the *comunidad indígena.* The indigenous community is based upon the organization of society previous to the arrival of the Spanish and the imposition of the hacienda. The original *ayllu* was a basic economic and social unit in the Incan social formation and many of these units were never broken up by haciendas. Data on the number and area of indigenous communities are difficult to obtain. Arturo Urquidi estimated the total number of *comuneros* in 1950 at roughly half of the rural population total for a figure of around 997,733 (1970, p. 147).[8]

Whatever the actual figures, the literature on the indigenous zones of the altiplano and valleys (especially the altiplano) reflects the importance of communal relationships even among peasants who may not be part of a recognized indigenous community. Of the Aymara population, Albó writes:

> In the middle of the apparent solitude of the Puna [the Aymara] could not live isolated. He lives submerged in his primary groups: the family and the community. He could neither make decisions, nor organize his work, nor have fun, nor pray if it is not in the reference to these relevant groups. Even his individualism . . . is manifested principally as a community egoism, of the group (1985, p. 8; my translation).

This "ideology of community" is found in, and reproduces in, the form of reciprocal labor arrangements as well as in the form of religious celebrations or rituals. "It is evident," writes Albó, "that the sentiment of reciprocity and group aid is one of the most developed Andean cultural themes" (1985, p. 14). The relationships within the process of production, which relied upon the indigenous ideology of community, include: *Faena,* a type of collective work, most often for some collective purpose, usually lasting one day; *Umaraqa,* a rotating system of collective labor for the benefit of one household and then for the next until all of the families of the group had received the help of all. The particular family being helped provided food and drink. In some provinces the group was limited to a few persons who worked in exchange for food. Also, the work was often followed with music, dance, and rituals; and *Achuqualla,* the ceremonial roofing of a new house, accompanied by many ritual elements. Other collective work arrangements involved organizing to build or repair a road, school, church, or to meet some natural disaster such as flooding. As well as labor for the benefit of the community there were work arrangements for the benefit of the authorities (i.e., servile labor performed as a labor obligation for which there was no return). These latter, servile arrangements were rapidly diminishing in the 1980s according to Albó (1985, pp. 14-23).

Furthermore, there were relationships of reciprocity between two individuals or among families. Chief among these relations was that of *ayni,* in which one form of service was returned in the exact same form of service. These services included exchanges of gifts, food, and drinks upon the occasion of a marriage, construction of a new house, and so forth. There were also obligations performed individually or in small groups of the community, one after the other, often over an extended period of time. A good example of this obligation was the *mit'a,* which was used by the Spanish as a means of extracting laborers from the rural communities for the mines. As a whole, these production relations benefited the nobility of the pre-Colombian period and was readily adapted by the Spanish to the labor needs in the mines, and by the hacendados to the labor needs of the hacienda. The primary point here is that these production relations reinforced and were enforced by the indigenous ideology of community. The relationships were legitimated by a priesthood that served to extract or alienate the "knowledge" of the direct form of the organization of the indigenous production process and that was reimposed in the form of moral or religious obligation. That is, to the laborer, his or her "duty" to the community (and nondirect producers) was sanctioned by religion.[9]

Because these labor exchange relationships existed within the entire Incan social formation, these same types of relationships existed among the Quechuas of the valleys as well as among the Aymaras described by Albó above. Arturo Urquidi notes that the relationship of the *ayni* (strict mutual reciprocity of labor) was found to exist among all indigenous peasants, not just among those living within indigenous communities (1970, p. 146). However, the valleys (and eastern Bolivia) had been affected by immigration to those areas (whereas the altiplano, except in the Lake Titicaca region, had been a zone of emigration). Some of these migrants entered class places defined by capitalist relations of production. As already noted, the indigenous population originally of the eastern zones was not agriculturalist and not in control of land.[10]

How significant is and what happens to members of this group who permanently migrate to other rural zones? The data on total permanent migration indicate that in 1976, 1,083,436 persons (or 28.6 percent of the population aged five years old or more) were living in a different province from the one in which they were born or living in 1971. Of that total, 62.5 percent had migrated sometime before 1971; 37.5 percent had changed provinces between 1971 and 1976. Given that the datum for the period previous to 1971 extends for an indefinite period and the latter for only the most recently available five years, it is probably safe to conclude that the annual rate of migration has been greatly increasing in recent history (Casanovas 1981, p. 18). Although, the permanent rural migrant had left the relations of the indigenous community and must be concerned directly with the survival of his or her own family, he or she did not necessarily enter into capitalist relations of production.

Compared to other Latin American countries, rural-rural permanent migration in Bolivia was a fairly significant portion of total migration. This fact was indicated in the Bolivian 1976 census, where 24 percent of those who had migrated also indicated that they had gone from a rural area to another rural area (Table III.5 in Casanovas 1981, p. 53).[11] Many of the rural-rural permanent migrants were considered to be "pioneer migrants" because they had moved into and established farms in territory that previously had been unfarmed and sparsely populated. The areas where these migrants moved to were mostly the colonization zones of the tropical (lower) valleys and the tropical plains of eastern Bolivia. According to Steve Wiggins, about 57,000 Bolivian families in the last quarter century had left their lands on the altiplano and Andean valleys to colonize regions in the tropical lowlands:

> Despite the opportunities for developing commercial agriculture in the tropics, the majority of the colonies are populated by *campesinos* from the highlands who lack capital and experience to take advantage of the opportunities. Using agricultural practices that cause the natural resources to deteriorate, these farmers cannot cultivate more than a few hectares and produce small harvests. They have to move frequently looking for virgin lands, because after three or four years the land does not produce as well as when virgin. Consequently, family production is small and the pioneer remains in poverty (1976, p. iii; my translation).

In 1976, Wiggins estimated the annual flow to the "colonies" to be around 2,500 families. With reports of families giving up and returning to their place of origin, it is difficult to gauge the total social significance of this form of migration. However this form of migration was important to the extent that many of these colonizers or pioneers, according to Wiggins, ended up offering their labor to the few large agricultural enterprises that had made it a practice to take over the land that the pioneers had cleared, used, and left. This practice would be extremely important because, to the extent that it occurred, it broke the traditional practices and social organization of the original *campesinos* who came to the land. Of course, it is also true that those families (or heads of households) who were willing to leave their original family's land had already distinguished themselves—in the same way as those who went looking for permanent wage work in the city or country—as people who had made the decision (or had no alternative but) to break the ties to their ancestral land and, in effect, leave the *indígena* side of the social formation.

Also, for various historical reasons, the Quechua of the Cochabamba valleys were more active in their own markets and more aggressive in organizing themselves against the hacendados than were the Aymaras. This resulted in their *sindicatos* being the most strongly organized in 1953 and simultaneously more readily able to negotiate with (and be co-opted by) the MNR and Barrientos regimes. In effect, the Quechuas tended to be more outward looking, which after the agrarian reform meant that they were more likely to participate in the marketplace and in the Bolivian state apparatuses than were the Aymaras.[12]

Further, it was in the Cochabamba area of the Chapare (an area of "colonization") where *campesinos* had taken advantage of the market conditions in coca leaf created by the foreign demand for cocaine. Even in this case, though, coca tended to be cultivated in small plots by small-holding peasantry susceptible to the same religious ideas and labor relationships of peasants elsewhere. That is, even though this was a uniquely lucrative activity for *campesinos*, they were not individually expanding production beyond what could be worked with family labor. When extra labor was needed, it was had through *ayni*.[13] With degrees of variation, the small, independent agricultural producer (i.e., indigenous peasant) remained within the ideological structure of the indigenous mode of production. That is, as demonstrated in the use of *ayni* by the migrant, and his or her continued adherence to the "cult of the *Pachamama*" (and consequent sacred regard for the land), even the coca leaf cultivator of the Chapare remained *indígena* (though in close proximity to a market articulation with international capitalism). Although the numbers and the significance are difficult to ascertain, there had to be some degree of leakage as some *indígenas* permanently entered class places defined by capitalist relations of production.

Regarding the segment of the indigenous population that had crossed to the urban areas of Bolivia, Albó points out that this group remained ideologically ("culturally") bound to the indigenous community. Albó found that the Aymaran migrants in the city remained rooted in the *campo,* maintaining a large network of social connections with members of their *comunidad,* as well as with the relatives who remained there:

> No matter the level or status the migrant reached in the city, he or she never completely separated from his *comunidad*. His or her place of origin was the point of reference for spiritual and material survival, for reproducing him or herself, and for coping with urban problems (1987, p. 6; my translation).

The key to understanding the phenomenon of the continuation of the urban migrants' links to the *campo* is probably found in the weak capitalist development, and consequent lack of class places, within the capitalist mode of production. It is wrong to assume that because the *indígena* had entered the urban environment, he or she was thus automatically inserted into the capitalist economy qua occupants of a capitalist mode class places. In his study of the indigenous population in the city of La Paz, Albó found that within the network of relations of the urban-dweller[14] to the rural community existed a type of articulation that relied upon and existed within a noncapitalist framework. Goods, money, and labor power circulated both ways between the city and the *campo* (1987, p. 39).

The study also found that 28 percent of the total informants maintained land in their place of origin. This group in particular reported strong social connections with their relatives and members of the *comunidad* and expected to eventually return to their community to make use of their land (1987, p. 8). Further, those without land continued to expect to gain land in the *campo* someday: "More than two thirds (69 percent) of those migrants without their own land continued to expect to have access to land in the community of origin" (1987, p. 8). For these reasons, the CIPCA team found that, except for the relatively few who had found a place in the capitalist economy and had improved their "status" relative to that of their position in the *campo,* most of the indigenous population in the city of La Paz continued to identify themselves with their community of origin. This led to the conclusion that at least in the city of La Paz the indigenous population constituted a separate culture within the city.[15]

Important to the analysis of "class place" here is the fact that the urban indigenous population maintained (to a significant degree) its own economic relations of exchange within its own "network" of economic and ideological relations. At one level, as Albó observed, the existence of this indigenous network indicated the precarious living conditions in both the rural and urban areas. At another level, the network indicated a partial articulation between the capitalist mode of production and the indigenous mode of production as the capitalist side of the city was able to make use of the services of the indigenous "community." Again, however, as in the case of the rural-rural migrant, leakage from one mode into the other was bound to occur as some former peasants found their new "place" within the capitalist side both economically and ideologically.

Seasonal migration, as discussed in Chapter 5, was less exposed and/or susceptible to the "benefits" of capitalist relations of production than might be expected from their seasonal participation in those relations. As noted in the previous chapter, Javier Albó considered the possibility that the experience of these social agents who occupy two class places would induce social change by introducing the worker to "scientific methods" of agriculture and oblige the worker to live for a time outside the social relations of the indigenous zone. One major obstacle to such a development, however, was that capitalist landowners tended to hire seasonal workers outside the legally defined contractual requirements of wage laborers. This meant that besides minimal returns to workers in economic terms, they had very little, if any, positive experience with capitalist relations that might presumably induce them to introduce innovation in social relations in the indigenous zones.

INDIGENOUS NONPRODUCERS

The labor relationships, which served to appropriate surplus value to the two classes of nonproducers in the Incan social formation, lent themselves to the continuation of a class of intermediaries between the ruling class of the capitalist mode of production and the direct producers of the indigenous mode of production. In the Colonial and Republican periods, this class place of intermediaries was defined by its use of "mental labor" to bring about the transfer of surplus value from the indigenous mode of production to the capitalist mode of production. The primary need of the capitalist state in the Bolivian social formation after the 1952 revolution, however, was not the extraction of surplus value (although this was provided in the form of seasonal migration and food production made available to the urban areas from the indigenous mode of production to the capitalist mode via a network of markets). Rather, the important function required of the *indígena* following the revolution was the political support of (and participation in) the repressive apparatus of the state against the miners. This resulted in the attempt of the Bolivian state to incorporate the functional equivalent of the state apparatus of the indigenous mode of production (i.e., the *sindicatos*) into the Bolivia state structure. The class place of intermediaries between the two modes of production was filled by the particular social agents who occupied the leadership positions of the peasant *sindicatos*. As described in Chapter 4, this attempt by the Bolivian state was successful until the Banzer years of the 1970s. Since the 1970s, with the development of the *katarista* movement and the birth of the CSUTCB, this class place has, in effect, been recaptured by the indigenous mode of production. That is, the significance of *katarismo,* and particularly of the CSUTCB, was the dissolution of the class place held by intermediary agents of the indigenous mode of production from the state apparatus of the capitalist side.

Put another way, in terms of definition of class place, the "political" element of this class place shifted from a domination of the indigenous direct producer by the capitalist mode of production to a relation of domination within the indigenous mode of production. This class place remained separate from the class place defined by the economic element of direct production and political element of subordination (i.e., the class place of the peasant); however, political domination shifted from a legitimation, which was previously enforced by the ideological element pertaining to the capitalist side, to a political domination legitimated and ultimately enforced by the ideological element pertaining to the indigenous side.

Clearly the shift of this intermediary class place did not occur by forces exclusively from the indigenous mode of production. Rather, the shift occurred in the historical context of the articulation of the two modes of production at the political and economic levels. The particular social agents themselves gained and developed their ideology from their contact with the urban environment and the capitalist mode of production. The political justification for the shift (i.e., the "awareness" of the indigenous peasant that was required to make the shift) existed in the experience on the part of the social agents involved of the articulation of the two modes of production at the economic level. Possibly one of the most important outcomes of the seasonal labor migration—the occupation of two class places by a single social agent—may have been the "awakening" of the direct producers to the contradiction that their "way of life" was indeed at risk. While the rural-rural seasonal migrant may not have learned the techniques of capitalist agriculture, he or she was exposed to the "knowledge" of the direct expropriation of his or her labor by the capitalist side.

It was also the case that the leaders of the *katarista* movement and the CSUTCB had at least been exposed to the urban environment. As noted in Chapter 4, the *katarista* movement began among students in the city of La Paz, and the urban areas of La Paz and Oruro tended to be the centers of strongest support for the *katarista* movement and the CSUTCB. Rivera makes the point that the "growing interaction between the cultural movement [nascent *katarismo*] of the urban residents and the syndicalist movement of the altiplano constituted one of the fundamentals of the rapid initial success of the *katarista* proposal and contributed to the downfall of the pro-Barrientos *caudillos* at the Congreso de Potosí in 1971" (1984, p. 128).[16]

To fill out the category of indigenous nonproducers there is the category of *comerciantes*. Just as there was a leadership group that was defined by its political domination between the capitalist and noncapitalist mode of production, an urban-dwelling commercial group was defined (or made distinct) by its nonproductive economic function. According to Bolivian census data the category of *servicios, comerciales, sociales y personales* increased from 8.2 percent of the economically active population in 1950 to 18.9 percent in 1976. This increase would seem to indicate that a sizable number of former *colonos* took the opportunity of the 1953 reform to take part in commercial activities.

IDEOLOGICAL UNIFICATION

The direct producers discussed earlier—the peasants, permanent rural, seasonal rural, and even urban migrants—represent a probable continuation, for the most part (more among some than others), of indigenous relations of production. The meaning of this is that indigenous ideology continued to be reflected and reproduced in economic practices of the indigenous population. In this direction lies the justification for referring to an indigenous population as a separate, competing, and largely homogenous category (i.e., direct producers of an indigenous mode of production). Furthermore, as argued above, the CSUTCB represented a political intermediary group whose ideological loyalty was to that indigenous group and in contradiction to the Bolivian state.

With the exception of the *comerciantes*,[17] the indigenous population could be considered, from a structural view, to be a political whole. Added to the social relations argument is the economic consideration that social agents of the indigenous side of the Bolivian formation bore direct economic exploitation by the capitalist side. That is, most direct beneficiaries of the process of appropriation of surplus value from the indigenous mode of production were within the dominant (or capitalist) side of the Bolivian social formation. For these two reasons it is plausible to contend that the peasantry, indigenous urban migrant, as well as seasonal and permanent rural migrant, should be politically united. That is, there is something of an organic class alliance here made possible by the shared ideological element.

However, given the ambiguity of the effects of long-term living in pioneer communities or urban settings on the ideological and economic practices of the indigenous population, there is still enough room to argue that Bolivian society is on its way to becoming capitalist. That is, the "pockets" of indigenous zones will gradually decline as the population is taken into the urban setting or shown the advantages of capitalist farming. To deepen the argument regarding the lasting importance of ideology in a noncapitalist mode of production (and explain why they can be slow to disappear without the use of outright violence), we need to also consider the undominated position ideology has in a noncapitalist mode of production.

SPECIAL CONDITION OF IDEOLOGY
IN NONCAPITALIST MODE OF PRODUCTION

As discussed in Chapter 2, a possible structural explanation for the assertion of this organic alliance on the basis of a shared ideological element results from the fact that noncapitalist modes of production are characterized by ideological and political processes that are not dominated (or determined within) the immediate processes of production (the economic element). Another way of explaining the problematic here is to view it in terms of the presence of extra-economic coercion. That is, economic activity may be performed for ideological or political purposes rather than the opposite. Whereas ideology in a capitalist mode of production is subordinated to the immediate process of production, in noncapitalist modes of production ideology is unbound. This undominated characteristic of ideology implies that the reproduction of the noncapitalist ideology in Bolivia was not dependent upon a complete continuation of indigenous relations of production (though that ideology—manifested in ideological practices, including reciprocity in the production process—would, to speak metaphorically, tend to seek to reproduce a production process in sympathy with its own conditions for existence).

Historically, the production process of the indigenous mode of production in Bolivia was directed by the state and ideology. Indigenous production relied upon the intervention of political coercion and/or ideological coercion rather than economic coercion. Or, that is, the state and its ideological practices directed, in effect, the production process for the sake of reproducing the conditions for the continuation of the ideological apparatus (state), rather than (as in a capitalist mode of production) for the sake of reproducing conditions for the expansion of capital. Ideology, then, was effectively in possession of its own "relative" autonomy vis-a-vis the production process. The relations of production and the production process were shaped by ideology, not vice versa.

This characteristic should alert us to the structural underpinning of the arguments made by representatives of the *katarista* movement in Bolivia. This helps us a great deal in explaining that just as Bolivian indigenous ideology—reciprocity and sacred consideration of the earth—was not conducive to real subsumption to capitalist relations of production, *indígenas* who were the bearers of this ideology and who had, for example, seasonally entered into capitalist relations of production were resistant and reactive to the ideological demands of those class places. The *katarista* movement in Bolivia was one indication not simply of a passive resistance, but a reaction to the experience of capitalism. Whereas, generally speaking, certain political and ideological arrangements may be conducive to the intrusion and internal development of capitalist relations of production, the ideology of the indigenous population in Bolivia was used in the 1970s and 1980s as the basis of political justification to resist capitalist relations of production and exploitation.[18]

TIN MINERS

The class alliance that was not so organic was that, which was attempted, between the above set of classes ("the *campesinado*") and the miners. Although the 1986 political thesis of the CSUTCB declared its support of its "brother" miners, there were numerous leaders of the *katarista* movement (as well as reports of leadership within the CSUTCB) who objected to the use of *campesinado* "political resources" being used to support a group whose way of life and consequent interests were separate from those of the *campesinado*. To a large extent the issue had become moot by 1986 and the decimation of the mining population brought about by the "tin crisis." In any event, because both the *campesinado* and the miners (and other urban working class) were exploited—the one through the articulation centered at the marketplace (and labor migration), the other through the direct appropriation of surplus value in the production process—there was a logic to the formation of an alliance between the *campesinado* and the miners (i.e., working class).

However, in terms of numbers, economic importance to the Bolivian social formation, and political importance, the *campesinado* far outweighed the Bolivian working class. Realizing the increasing structural need of the capitalist side of the Bolivian social formation for an expansion of capitalist development in Bolivian agriculture, the Bolivian state began to rethink its policy toward the indigenous zones of the *campo* in the early 1980s.

BOLIVIAN STATE AND STATE POLICY

Making use of Poulantzas on this subject: "the principal role of the state apparatuses is to maintain the unity and cohesion of a social formation by concentrating and sanctioning class domination, and in this way reproducing social relations or class relations" (1978, p. 24). The state itself is a "condensation" of existing class relations. Particular regimes occupy states much in the way that social agents occupy class places. The state itself is already structured by the confluence of class relations.

In the Bolivian case, the state was structured by its location among class relations resulting from its place in an international capitalist economy, the

Bolivian national capitalist class, and the articulation of the Bolivian capitalist mode of production with the indigenous mode of production. Primary to this analysis is the nature of the points of articulation between the two modes of production. As depicted above, the Bolivian state itself was part of the creation of the class place of the intermediary class. That is, the intermediary class place, which had existed in some form since the Incan polity, had traditionally been directly legitimated by, if not directly part of, the state apparatus. The Bolivian state was structurally required to maintain this intermediary class place because of the social formation's structural articulation with the indigenous mode of production at the economic level. This structural requirement incumbent upon the state was a function of the state's role of maintaining cohesion of the social formation.

Unable to reach into the ideological apparatus of the indigenous side itself, the state accomplished the task of keeping the social formation cohesive through the establishment, in effect, of an intermediary class place that, except when recaptured by the indigenous side, could be defined by its participation in the political apparatus.[19] Because this "intermediary class' was at least partially constituted by the Bolivian state, the state itself became a focus of the conflict between the indigenous mode and the capitalist mode. In recent history, the cohesive role of the state became increasingly tenuous after the death of General René Barrientos.

As discussed in Chapter 4, the primary objective of state policy immediately following the agrarian reform was to incorporate the leadership of the peasant sindicatos into its own political and repressive apparatuses. Economic development (i.e., capitalist development) was pursued or fostered with roads and easy credit policies mostly in the Santa Cruz region. With the decline in tin export as a source of revenue, the Bolivian state began to reconsider its attitude of neglect toward the indigenous zones in the mid-1980s.

In seeking to increase agricultural production the state faced at least three major problems. First, there was the contradiction that would need to be overcome in which the increase in volume of products for the domestic market (as a result of expanded capitalist farming) would lower the price of agricultural products and thus provide a further disincentive for market participation by the peasantry. That is, an increase in production would simultaneously drive the *campesinado* out of the marketplace. This would mean that the state would have to concentrate on a few products (i.e., products that would not compete for domestic consumption). As discussed in Chapter 5, this policy was tried in the Santa Cruz region and met with two problems: fluctuating world market prices that would not compensate the cost of production and the consequent shortage of labor at a wage low enough to produce for the world price.

The second overall problem faced by the state was that the nature of the relations of production and the ideology that existed among the *campesinado* was not conducive to capitalist (commercial) agriculture. The third problem was that because the majority of the Bolivian population was located within the indigenous zones of production, a reliable cheap labor supply was difficult to obtain. That is, to the extent that the *campesinado* of the indigenous zones could reproduce themselves without providing labor power directly in the capitalist side, they inhibited capitalist development both in those zones and in the rest of Bolivia.

From the state's point of view the solution to these three problems lay in the breakup of the indigenous zones of noncapitalist production. This task was made difficult by, first, the overall weak development of capitalism in Bolivia. Bolivia had little internal source of capital for investment; a problem that was compounded by a $4 billion debt and declaration of default. (The Paz Estenssoro government attempted to overcome this problem by actively inviting foreign investment.) Second, this task was made politically difficult by the development of *katarismo* and the recapture by the indigenous side of the intermediary class place discussed above. Nonetheless, in the mid-1980s, the Paz government was attempting to finesse a way of introducing large-scale production to the indigenous zones.

One attempt was through an increase in rural property tax, which was proposed in the *"Reforma Tributaria"* law of 1986. Placing a rural property tax on individual owners of property would have at least two advantages for the state. One, if properly carried out (and this was the vision of the law), the records of property titles held by the ministry of agriculture and peasantry (MACA) would be computerized and used to enforce not just the collection of taxes but also force people off of land the title for which had never been processed by MACA. Second, those *campesinos* who were not engaged in the market to the degree that they could have the money to pay the tax would have to forfeit their property. The major problem with such a law was that the Bolivian government did not have the resources to enforce it. Third, any attempt to enforce the forfeiture of land would invite active resistance from the organized *campesinado*.

The Bolivian government realized in the 1980s that it would need the cooperation of the *campesino* organizations (particularly the CSUTCB) to bring about change in the *campo*. To obtain this cooperation, at the same time reshaping the nature of production in the indigenous zones, the Paz government put forth its plan of action that it called *Agropoder* (Agropower). Previous to the introduction of this plan, the CSUTCB had introduced for public debate its own plan for rewriting the 1953 Agrarian Reform law, that it labeled the *Proyecto de Ley Agraria Fundamental*. In a forum sponsored by the *Instituto Latinoamericano de Investigaciones Sociales* (ILDIS), Victor Hugo Cardenas, a representative of the

CSUTCB and leader of the Movimiento Revolucionario Tupaj Katari—Liberación (MRTK-L), argued that the 1953 Reform "was a proposal for developing capitalism, in the logic of constructing material bases for a liberal bourgeois society and state in which the *campesino* is transformed into an individual private property owner; this is the logic of 'one citizen, one vote' that does not recognize the preexisting reality, not only on the altiplano, but also in the valleys and the east" (ILDIS September 1985, p. 27). In response to the CSUTCB proposal, which emphasized reorganizing the peasantry in an "expanded" or more general form of the *comunidades*, the Paz government proposed the creation of Centros Operativos del Agropoder (COAs), with which to impose capitalist relations (with the help of conscripts from the army) in the indigenous zones.

At the heart of the dispute was the cooperation that the government could obtain from the peasant leadership. That is, the state had to seek to recapture the intermediary class. However, the apparent strength of the *katarista* movement and the continuation of noncapitalist relations of production in the indigenous zones made that recapture difficult and a potential site of conflict. The government's "Agropoder" plan was denounced by the CSUTCB at its 1986 Conference in Sucre: "We seek the destruction of the state apparatus that intends to implement "Agropoder" as a mechanism to serve the interest of the new *latifundistas* and private businesspeople (*Resoluciones del VIII ampliado de la CSUTCB 1986*, section from the *Politico-Sindico* commission; also see section from the Economic Commission).

Probably the most important point here is that, by definition, the Bolivian state is a capitalist state (shaped by the domination of capitalist class relations) and cannot, by definition, switch to policies that would be favorable in terms of surplus value extraction to the indigenous side. It will no doubt attempt to win the current battle by attempting to co-opt the CSUTCB leadership. The CSUTCB leadership itself will either allow this co-optation (perhaps without recognizing it as such), striking the best bargain they can, or realize that this is a battle that cannot be won as long as the Bolivian state remains the "Bolivian state."

CONCLUSION

Despite attempts of the Bolivian state to the contrary, the capitalist revolution of 1952 had not and could not mobilize the *campesinado* to an idea of profit-making and capital expansion. However, the capitalist side of the Bolivian social formation was able to make use of the *campesinado* at two significant points of articulation between the capitalist and indigenous modes of production: seasonal labor migration and the extraction of surplus food production via the marketplace. If only by sheer size, it was the *campesinado* and not the urban worker who, as a group, was and would be the primary key to setting the direction of Bolivian development.

After the breakup of the hacienda system of labor control (and because the original complete Incan formation had long since been vitiated), the *campesinado* was, in effect, "structurally free" to persist in noncapitalist behavior and/or create new relations of production in the *campo*. These new structures of production could originate in the dialectic of the pressure of the capitalist side on the noncapitalist side. The primary issues of who controlled arable land and for what purpose continued as a political expression of the underlying ideological contradictions in the Bolivian social formation.

NOTES

1. The *katarista* movement is discussed in Chapter 4.
2. Of course, the document is a "political document." As pointed out below, the document itself is part of a political/ideological attempt to create a new consciousness of political awareness and "position."
3. The *katarista* movement and the political parties and the CSUTCB that emerged from it are covered in Chapter 4.
4. It is also true, as discussed earlier, that if an indigenous person did enter the capitalist mode, he or she could well cast off the identity and designation of "indio" (and by extension that identity, I am labeling *indígena*).
5. Although, it can be argued that racism was necessary for a production process that relied upon the "sub-human" status of the indian (i.e., without civil rights) such as in the production process of hacienda.
6. "Ideological mirage" refers to the usage of "ideology" as something inherently false (or nonvalid); in this case, something not based in the process of production.
7. Those delineations are described in Chapter 5.
8. Since the 1800s the data on property holdings have not distinguished members of indigenous communities from individual land holders. For the purposes of the 1953 Agrarian Reform, while the territories of indigenous communities were recognized as belonging to specific communities, the property was considered to have been divided up by the individual families.
9. As discussed in Chapter 3, this "knowledge" of production was in effect extracted by the priesthood who, in turn, represented (i.e., re-presented) the knowledge of production to the direct producer in terms of a cosmology of gods that needed to be addressed in rituals and which oversaw the fertility of the earth and the success of the cultivation and harvest.
10. I do not mean to minimize the situation of the eastern tribal groups. These people, some of whom continued in hunting and gathering groups (which were being ideologically penetrated and broken up by protestant missionaries in the 1980s), were decimated with the remainder brought into capitalist relations (often "debt peonage") of

production. See Reister's works on the Santa Cruz region for a description of the tragic conditions confronting the remaining indigenous tribal groups.

11. The 44.3 percent indicated that they had migrated from rural areas to urban areas.

12. Ironically, it was this very use of the marketplace and their expectation of being able to use the state to control prices of consumer goods (such as flower, rice, sugar, and coffee) that led to the immediate cause of the Cochabamba Valley massacres in 1974. This event marked the beginning of the shift away from the Bolivian state as it revealed a fundamental contradiction in political relationship of the Quechuan *campesinado* and the capitalist state. See discussion in Chapter 4.

13. My information regarding coca production in the Chapare was obtained from an informant whose family farmed noncoca products in the Chapare, but who did engage in the commercial activity of buying coca leaf from farmers for sale to the producers of the coca paste. It is unquestionably true that the Chapare became something of a hotbed of commercial activity with the high inflow of coca dollars to the residents who cultivated coca and to the producers of the coca paste. The producers, who employed labor that had migrated in from all sections of Bolivia, had indeed become capitalists; and the workers—paid to stomp the leaf—had indeed become workers. According to stories in the Bolivian press these workers were generally young and often were users of the coca paste to help alleviate the boredom of the stomping and pain of the sores on their feet and ankles (caused by the chemicals used in the processing of the coca leaf to coca paste). I would guess that these workers, if they were lucky, returned to their places of origin after accumulating some savings with which to aid in the reproduction of their family and community of origin. If they were not lucky, as an easily replaceable resource to the producers, they were simply discarded after becoming too unhealthy to continue working and were left to an uncertain fate. Although I cannot show a direct link, during my stay in Cochabamba in 1986 there was an increasing number of homeless adolescents who made their livelihood by offering the refined coca paste for sale in the streets. According to press reports, agencies that were designed to provide shelter for homeless children found that many of these adolescents were addicted to cocaine (coca paste).

14. See Albó (1982, *Chukiyawu; la cara aymara de la Paz; Una odisea: buscar "pega,"* p. 190) for breakdown and trends in type of occupation engaged in by migrants to La Paz. As of 1976, the last year of data, the percentage of migrants from the *campo* in the "modern sector" of "manufacturing, public and private employment" had declined to around 15 percent. Around 34 percent were in the "traditional sector" of artisans and *comerciantes*. The percentage in the miscellaneous category of masons, porters, and those shifting from one unskilled job to another was a steeply rising 42 percent.

15. It is also perhaps revealing to note (as does Albó) that the site of the city of La Paz was an Incan urban center before the arrival of the Spanish. That is, *Chukiyawu* existed before "La Paz."

16. The development of the *Katarista* movement is covered in some detail in Chapter 4.

17. The *comerciantes*, involved in buying and marketing of indigenous products, gained economically from their class location in the market doorway between the indigenous side and the capitalist side of the social formation. In a similar way, the leadership

Production, Class, and Ideology 125

group was marked by its political power, located in the political doorway of articulation between the two sides.

18. This point is drawn out in the conclusion.

19. By "political apparatus" I mean state (or state supported) bureaucracies (e.g., the structure of the CNTCB).

Chapter 7
Conclusions

This chapter presents the major conclusions of this study and, in support of those conclusions, briefly summarizes the structural interpretation of Bolivian history presented in the previous chapters. The primary focus of the previous historical analysis is the point of political articulation between the noncapitalist mode of production of the indigenous side and the precapitalist/capitalist mode of production of the *criollo* side of the Bolivian social formation. Reviewing the major features of the political articulation, the present chapter considers the stated political objectives of the CSUTCB in the 1980s and potential state response.

The major conclusion of this study is that the ideological processes of the indigenous mode of production are in contradiction with the logic of the development of capitalist relations of production. By "logic of development" is meant a series or set of conditions that determines the requirements of further conditions. Or, vice versa, a condition cannot exist or "hold true" without the existence of other conditions. In the same way, we can speak of a logic (e.g., the process of the development or reproduction of capitalist relations) of production. The process is a complex whole of certain conditions. We, as observers of the process of articulation between capitalist and noncapitalist modes of production, can speak of conditions not being met and/or conditions of one process that contradict (or exclude) necessary conditions of the other process. This contradiction is at the heart of a political disarticulation of the two modes of production that characterize the Bolivian social formation.

The most important factor affecting the stability of the Bolivian social formation is the contradiction posed by indigenous ideological processes in the articulation of the two modes of production. Chapter 2 presents the argument that ideology in a noncapitalist mode of production is not ultimately determined by the economic process. The production process in a noncapitalist mode of production, instead, can be affected and ultimately determined by ideological and/

or political processes. The ideology of the indigenous side of the social formation, although in a dialectical relationship with indigenous relations of production, is not created within and is not bounded by the "immediate process of production." Unlike the situation of a capitalist mode of production, indigenous ideology is reproduced in the general process of reproduction of the mode of production. In effect, in a noncapitalist mode of production, the immediate process of production does not exist. It does not make sense to speak either of processes external or internal to an immediate process of production within the whole process of social reproduction. The noncapitalist mode of production brings to bear its noneconomic elements on the process of production (the success of which leads to the reproduction of the mode of production). In a capitalist mode of production, it makes sense to speak of the existence of an "immediate process of production" in which the economic element is surrounded by something of a conceptual barrier from those elements that are then "external" to the immediate process of production, but are part of the general production and reproduction process.

The genius of Poulantzas' analysis of a capitalist mode of production is that he demonstrated, in effect, that the immediate process of production was not simply the economic. Rather, within the dynamics of the immediate production process, the economic element of production shaped ideological and political relations within it. (These ideological and political relations were then used by Poulantzas to define his version of the "new petty bourgeoisie.") This production process can be seen to operate within a larger shell of ideological and political processes some of which may be noncapitalist processes. However, the existence of the immediate capitalist process itself would indicate that these noncapitalist ideologies were either conducive or benign to the development of capitalist relations of production. Over time we might well expect that the ideologies conducive to the social relations of the immediate process of production would become pervasive and predominant as fewer and fewer social agents could occupy class places (or, perhaps, nonclass areas)[1] unaffected by the capitalist process of production.[2]

The argument here, then, is that within the immediate process of production the economic process of production entails the creation of political and ideological processes. Further, capitalism subordinates political and ideological practices outside the immediate process of production to its economic logic. The logic of this economically dominated production process involves the maximization of surplus value for the recreation of conditions for the maximization of surplus value. This is not true of noncapitalist modes of production; the process of production is not dominated by the economic element of the process. The economic element, to speak metaphorically, is not unleashed; rather, the logic of the production process is affected by, and ultimately determined by, ideological and political practices.

Another way of presenting this last point is to speak of the articulation of capitalist relations of production with noncapitalist ideological and political processes. The vision presented here is that capitalist modes are basically contained within the immediate process of production. Areas outside of the immediate process either conform to its logic (articulate with capitalist relations of production) or "wither away." For example, this could be used to explain the situation of the feudal state apparatus of the Catholic Church. With the development of capitalism the Catholic Church did not wither away, but its dominance in the state apparatus did. Further, the occupation of Catholic priest became an ambiguous one (not subject to ready capitalist capture).

This theoretical analysis has two significant implications for the analysis here of the political and ideological processes in Bolivia. First, the reproduction of ideological practices of the indigenous mode of production is not adversely affected by social agents who seasonally enter capitalist relations of production. Second, indigenous ideology is most vulnerable, perhaps paradoxically, not at the economic level of articulation but at the sites of ideological practices. That is, if noncapitalist ideology is logically dominant to economic processes, ideological practices and not relations of production is the logically primary area of contention. This means that (short of a violent elimination of indigenous relations of production) the primary area of attack for the Bolivian state, in the implementation of capitalist production processes, should be the ideological practices of the indigenous side.[3]

A second major finding or conclusion of the study is that the articulation in Bolivia between a capitalist mode and a noncapitalist mode of production has resulted in a class place that I have defined by its political domination of the direct producers of the indigenous mode of production. The key question in an analysis of this class is from which side of the formation the social agents who occupy this class place receive their grant of legitimacy. The only source from which the legitimacy can come over a consistent period of time is the indigenous side. Yet, the state, as it has historically, must seek to maintain political domination of the indigenous population. When the state has not been able to extract voluntary cooperation, such as during the *pacto militar,* the state has relied upon repressive force that periodically has been challenged by indigenous rebellions. The logically (and historically) inescapable contradiction regarding this ideological grant of legitimacy is that it has to come from the indigenous side (or else the social agents lose their ability to convince the indigenous population to do what the state needs them to do); however, when the grant comes from the indigenous side (as it did in the 1980s), that grant required the social agents in that intermediary class place to pull the indigenous population further from a politically or economically cooperative relationship with the state. I flesh out the above discussion by summarizing the history of this structural contradiction.

Bolivian resident and scholar Javier Albó recently noted that two centuries ago, in 1781, the city of La Paz was blockaded by a ring of thousands of Aymaras led by Julián Apasa (Tupác Katari). Nearly two centuries later, in December 1979, the *gente decente* of La Paz perhaps relived something of the panic of their forebearers as the *indiada* ("indian mass") once again blockaded the city in protest over economic measures implemented by the government (in Stern 1987, p. 379). Once again, perhaps for just a moment in the temporary isolation caused by the blockade, the *criollo* population perceived the vulnerability of a society that existed upon an alien land. Such a moment of disarticulation was, however, only a moment.

The arrival of the Spanish to the Andes in the 1590s resulted in the figurative, if not literal, decapitation of the Incan social formation through the destruction of the Incan ruling class and its political apparatus. However, the *ayllu* and its leadership (as well as its ideological practices) remained intact even as it was required (through the Spanish political apparatus) to turn the same ideological practices to benefit the new ruling class on the Spanish (precapitalist) side of the new social formation. The direct producers of the *indígena* side occupied a class place that was dominated ideologically and politically before the Spanish arrived. With indigenous ideological practices left in place, the prevailing indigenous ideology remained in existence in conjunction with the continuation of relations of production, which were based in the economic arrangement of the *ayllu* or *comunidad*. The continued existence of this partially co-opted ideological apparatus helped assure that indigenous ideology was sufficient to drive periodic rebellions against the domination of the Spanish and the Bolivian ruling class of the Republic. The last major (and "successful") rebellion of the indigenous side was that which resulted in the 1953 agrarian reform.

In Chapter 3, which covers the structural history of Bolivia, I develop an analysis of the "structure" of the pre-1952 social formation. For the approximately two thirds of the indigenous population immediately previous to the agrarian reform of 1953, the hacienda system acted as a mechanism for attaching its labor power to the "capitalist" or *criollo* side of the formation. The nature of this tight articulation as demonstrated in Chapter 3 was such that neither noncapitalist relations of production nor ideological practices were eliminated. In fact, by relying upon and reinforcing the expansion of the absolute surplus value of the indigenous farmer, the hacienda system helped to maintain noncapitalist relations of production in the *campo*. This is to say that, unlike what many Bolivian state planners may have expected in the 1950s, the indigenous farmer was in no way structurally compelled or prepared for the development of capitalist farming. To the contrary, the "formal" nature of the subsumption of the indigenous labor process kept that process and (its concurrent ideology) largely intact. The argument regarding the nature of the subsumption of the indigenous labor to a capitalist mode during the period from the arrival of the Spanish to the 1953 land reform is drawn out in Chapter 3, where I contend that the hacienda's use of *indígena* labor should be seen as "formal subsumption" (i.e., the taking of a labor process as it is found and extracting labor surplus to the benefit of capital accumulation) to a capitalist mode of production.

The immediate and most dramatic impact of the 1953 agrarian reform was the legal ending of the tight articulation function of the hacienda. That is, the immediate structural result of that change was the initial separation of the two modes at the economic level. Following the 1953 reform, the *indígena* laborer was disattached from any processes of labor relating to the capitalist mode of production as long as he or she physically stayed in the *indígena* zone. Of course, many did not. Because of the lack of self-contained economic resources for expansion on the part of the *campesinado,* articulation between the capitalist side and the noncapitalist side continued—most notably in the form of migrant labor. However, capitalism remained largely an alien system. Left to its own devices, the *campesinado* became, for the most part, a class of small-holding argriculturalists tending to self-sufficiency, placing assured survival ahead of risk in the marketplace. Nonetheless, the Bolivian state of the capitalist side of the Bolivian social formation, acted from structural imperatives, especially after the decline of mining in the early 1980s, to displace the noncapitalist peasantry.

This attempt at displacement was not accepted by the indigenous peasantry. First, the *campesinado* perceived and countered the threat to its survival qua peasantry. Second, an alternative ideology existed that addressed its appeal directly to the peasantry as an ethnic group, if not a class, "exploited" by an alien economic and political system brought from the outside by the *blancos.* That is, there were two important aspects of the majority of the Bolivian peasantry. One, they were a peasantry in the "universal"[4] meaning of that word. Second, they had a historically unique ideology, which accounts for their demonstrated resistance to capitalism as well as being the basis for a political movement of the *indígena* against the economic and political "hegemony" of the dominant class.

As of the 1980s, the two modes of production were loosely articulated[5] at the economic level, separated (or disjointed) at the ideological level, and increasingly disarticulated at the political level as the intermediary class became occupied by social agents who moved themselves away from the state apparatus by seeking "legitimacy" not from the state but from the indigenous population. This kind of linkage, or articulation, between the modes made for a precarious political situation. In the mid-1980s, the Bolivian state was in the position of attempting to maintain a political articulation in which the ideological element of the subordinate mode was, in effect, pulling its mode further away from the capitalist mode. The principal area of this domination was at the political level, and it was there that this "pulling away" was manifested (or indicated by) the *katarista* movement in general and the leadership of the Confederación Sindical Unica de Trabajadores Campesinos de Bolivia (CSUTCB) in particular.

At its 1986 national meeting, the CSUTCB made clear its intentions to struggle against the Bolivian state policies of *Agropoder* and for the "transformation of the system and the installation of a worker's economic, political, and social model" (1986; from *Platforma de Lucha* of the Political Committee). Further, the same document called for the maintenance of political independence of the *campesino* movement and declared that "the only road that would conduct them to true national and social liberation was that indicated by our martyrs Tupác Katari, Bartolina Sisa, Tomás Katari, Alejo Calatayud, Toucha, Martin Ucho" (1986; from *Platforma de Lucha* of the Political Committee).

Historically, the Bolivian state has responded to the structural task of articulation by co-opting the *kuraka*. To the extent it was successful, it accomplished an economic and political domination of the indigenous mode of production. The Spanish and Bolivian states however were never able, despite the efforts of the Catholic Church, to eliminate the ideological practices[6] within the indigenous mode of production. Historically, this meant the indigenous side of the social formation remained capable of producing its own para-political apparatus (e.g., the CSUTCB) and its own political leadership that have periodically acted to overthrow the Spanish/Bolivian state.

In structural terms, the intermediary class place was the equivalent of the "supervisor" in Poulantzas' analysis of the production process in monopoly capitalism. However, whereas the "supervisor" gains his or her authority through the manipulation of the "knowledge" of the production process (e.g., the supervisor is carrying out the directions of the manager who "knows what is best"), the agents who occupied the class place of intermediary in Bolivia did not derive their legitimacy from an ideology that resulted from capitalist production processes. Rather, the class place (when not dependent upon the repressive apparatus of the state) was dependent upon the ideological reproduction processes of the indigenous mode of production.

The diagram that might be used to represent this class place at the mode of political and ideological articulation would have to demonstrate the ideological point of the indigenous mode intersecting the political apparatus of the capitalist side. However, that ideological process repelled the political apparatus of the capitalist mode. This repulsion can be at least partially explained by the fact that the capitalist mode did not have a strong "immediate process of production." The capitalist mode, dependent upon foreign capital, and its political apparatus, dependent upon foreign aid, was not capable of generating an ideology of the workplace that might, over time, pervade the social formation. Furthermore, the weakness of the capitalist side was complemented by the strength of the ideology of the *indígena,* which was inimical to the development of capitalist social relations. As the Bolivian state moved (or attempted to move in the 1980s) to implement rural property taxes and establish the COAs (discussed in Chapter 6), the *campesinado* was ideologically compelled to defend *indígena* relations of production. This combination of characteristics made for consistent conditions of political instability.

The state's objective of developing commercial agriculture in the *campo* in the 1980s depended upon the ideological recapture of the class place of the intermediary (e.g., the CSUTCB leadership). The key question is from which side of the formation did these social agents receive their legitimacy to rule? Part of the contradiction in this relationship is that when social agents of the intermediary class received their authority from the Spanish/Bolivian side they tended to lose the political support of the indigenous population. This occurred most recently with the shift of the *campesinado* away from the Confederación Nacional Trabajadores Campesinos de Bolivia (CNTCB) to the CSUTCB.[7]

Authority that depends upon the capitalist side either withers away or has to rely upon force (repressive apparatus of the state). Perhaps the only way for this "problem" to be solved from the point of view of the capitalist side was to penetrate and disrupt the indigenous relations and ideology of the production process. That is, the indigenous mode of production itself would have to be violently displaced (thus doing away with the need for a political intermediary class place).

As mentioned in Chapter 6, the state indicated that it might have just such a plan in mind when it proposed the use of military "conscripts" to assist the Centros Operativos del Agropoder (COAs). Assuming that the state was planning the use of military force, the CSUTCB denounced the use of military personnel of any kind in the *campo.* From its 1986 meeting, the published statement of the Political Committee maintained that the military would be used to guarantee the property rights of new *latifundistas.* Further, it commented that in other countries the same project as that called "COAs" in Bolivia would be called something like the "anti-subversion strategic hamlets program." The

1986 document goes on in this same section to argue that the state was attempting to return the "agricultural workers of Bolivia to a colonial style of exploitation" (1986, Section of Political Committee).

In fact, the state's more likely intent was not to reintroduce the feudallike conditions of the hacienda but to force the development of capitalist relations of production. Such a development, if it were possible, would undermine the class place of the peasant leadership, transform the *campesino* into a working class, and tie the *indígena* (qua rural workers and farmers) directly into political relations with the Bolivian state. Such a bold initiative on the part of the state would most likely have to be carried out with the use of violence as the indigenous population was bound to actively resist such a transformation.

NOTES

1. A nonclass area might be what once was a class place within a previous mode of production (e.g., Catholic priest).
2. This has to do with the conceptualization of an area external to the immediate process of production. This external area also involves class places that are structured by capitalist production processes. For example, the attorney (whose profession, unlike that of the priest, has grown with the development of capitalist relations of production) is located outside the immediate production process. But the activities of the attorney involve things that are essential to capitalist reproduction (e.g., the making and enforcement of contracts; and, more generally, the manipulation of ideas such that "right of private property" remains sanctified).
3. Such an "attack" could occur through the practices of missionaries and teachers of capitalist-conducive "knowledge."
4. By "universal peasant" is meant that categorization that is used to describe the common phenomenon of small-holding agriculturalist. For an extensive definition see Eric R. Wolf (1969).
5. "Tight articulation" is the on site fusion of corresponding elements of the "joined." "Loose articulation" is "joining" by way of spatial circulation of labor, ideas, or commodities from the "area" of one mode to that of another.
6. These practices (religious or otherwise) were directly related to relations of production and/or distribution. To eliminate the practices would mean eliminating the economic practices that characterized the indigenous mode of production (e.g., productive relations of reciprocity).
7. This shift is discussed in Chapter 4.

Bibliography

In addition to those works cited in the text, this bibliography includes writings that have been useful in shaping ideas for the book.

Aguillo, Frederico. 1985. *La inmigración extradepartmental en la ciudad de Cochbamba: Encuesta socio-antropologica (1984)*. Cochabamba: Universidad Mayor de San Simón, Editorial Universitaria.

Alberti, Giorgio, and Enrique Mayer, eds. 1974. *Reciprocidad e intercambio en los andes peruanos*. Lima: Instituto de Estudios Peruanos.

Albó, Javier. 1980. *Khitipxtanse: ¿quienes somos?* 2nd ed. La Paz: Centro de Investigación y Promoción del Campesinado (CIPCA).

―――. 1985. *Desafios de la solidaridad Aymara*. Cuaderno de Investigación, no. 25. La Paz: CIPCA.

―――. 1987. "From MNRistas to Kataristas to Katari." In *Resistance, Rebellion, and Consciousness in the Andean Peasant World: 18th to 20th Centuries,* ed. Steve J. Stern. Madison: Univ. Wisconsin Press.

Albó, Javier, and Josep Barnadas. 1985. *La cara campesina de nuestra historia*. La Paz: Unitas.

Albó, Javier, and Olivia Harris. 1986. *Monteras y Guardatojas: Campesinos y mineros en el Norte de Potosi*. Cuaderno de Investigación, no. 26. La Paz: Centro de Investigación y Promoción del Campesinado (CIPCA).

Albó, Javier, Tomás Greaves, and Godofredo Sandoval. 1981. *Chukiyawu: La cara aymara de La Paz.* vol. 1, *El paso a la ciudad.* Cuaderno de Investigación, no. 20. La Paz: Centro de Investigación y Promoción del Campesinado (CIPCA).

―――. 1982. *Chukiyawu: La cara aymara de La Paz. vol. 2, Una odiesae: buscar "pega"*. Cuaderno de Investigación, no. 22. La Paz: CIPCA.

―――. 1983. *Chukiyawu: La cara aymara de La Paz.* vol. 3, *Cabalgando entre dos mundos*. Cuaderno de Investigación, no. 24, La Paz: CIPCA.

―――. 1987. *Chukiyawu: La cara aymara de La Paz* vol. 4, *Nuevos lazos con el campo*. Cuaderno de Investicación, no. 29. La Paz: CIPCA.

Alexander, Robert. 1982. *Bolivia: Past, Present, and Future of its Politics*. New York: Praeger.

Althusser, Louis. 1984. *Essays on Ideology.* London: Verso.

Althusser, Louis, and Etienne Balibar. 1979. *Reading Capital*. Translated by Ben Brewster, London: Verso.

Anderson, Perry. 1979. *Lineages of the Absolutist State*. London: Verso.

Antezana, Ergueta. 1979. *Proceso y sentencia a la reforma agraria en Bolivia*. Colección luces y sombras, no. 1. La Paz: Puerta del Sol.

Antonio Mayorga, René. 1978. "National-Popular State, State Capitalist and Military Dictatorship in Bolivia: 1952-1975," *Latin American Perspectives* 5 (Spring):89-119.

Bastien, Joseph W. 1978. *Mountain of the Condor: Metaphor and Ritual in an Andean Ayllu*. American Ethnological Society, Monograph 64. St. Paul: West Publishing.

Calderon, Fernando, and Jorge Dandler, eds. 1984. *Bolivia: La fuerza historica del campesinado*. Cochabamba: Centro de Estudios de la Realidad Económica y Social (CERES) and United Nations Research Institute for Social Development (UNRISD).

Camacho Sua, Carlos. 1966. *Minifundia, Productivity, and Land Reform in Cochabamba*. Research Paper, no. 21. Madison: Land Tenure Center, Univ. Wisconsin.

Campbell, Leon G. 1987. "Ideology and Factionalism during the Great Rebellion." In *Resistance, Rebellion, and Consciousness in the Andean Peasant World: 18th to 20th Centuries*, ed. Steven J. Stern. Madison. Univ. Wisconsin Press.

Casanova, Roberto S. 1981. *Migración interna en Bolivia: origen, magnitud y principales caracteristicas*. La Paz: Ministerio de Trabajo.

Chilcote, Ronald H., and Dale L. Johnson, eds. 1983. *Theories of Development: Mode of Production or Dependency?* Beverly Hills: Sage.

Clark, Ronald J. 1968. "Land Reform and Peasant Market Participation in the Northern Highlands of Bolivia" *Land Economics* 44 (May):153-72.

Confederación Sindical de Unica de Trabajadores Campesinos de Bolivia (CSUTCB). 1984. *Tesis Politica, 1983. Published with Oprimidos pero no vencidos: Luchas del campesinado aymara y qhechwa, 1900-1980*. La Paz: CSUTCB and Instituto de Historia Social Boliviana (HISBOL).

———. 1986. *Resoluciones del VIII ampliado de la CSUTCB*. La Paz: CSUTCB.

Crabtree, John, Gavan Duffy, and Jenny Pearce. 1987. *The Great Tin Crash: Bolivia and the World Tin Market*. London: Latin American Bureau.

Dandler, Jorge. 1983. *Sindicalismo campesino en Bolivia: Cambios estructurales en Ucreña, 1935-1952*. (2nd ed.) Cochabamba: Centro de Estudios de la Realidad Económica y Social (CERES).

Dandler, Jorge, and Juan Torrico A. 1987. "From the National Indigenous Congress to the Ayopaya Rebellion: Bolivia, 1945-1947." In *Resistance, Rebellion, and Consciousness in the Andean Peasant World: 18th to 20th centuries*, ed. Steve J. Stern. Madison: Univ. Wisconsin Press.

DeJanvry Alaine, and Lynn Ground. 1978. "Types and Consequences of Land Reform in Latin America," *Latin American Perspectives* 5 (Fall):90-112.

Dieterich, Heinz. 1982. "Some Theoretical and Methodological Observations about the Inca Empire and the Asiatic Mode of Production," *Latin American Perspectives* 9 (Fall): 111-32.

Doria Medina, Samuel. *La economia informal en Bolivia*. La Paz: Published by author.

Dorsey, J. 1975. *A Case Study of the Lower Cochabamba Valley: Ex-Haciendas Parotani and Caranares*. Research Paper, no 64.

Dunkerley, James. 1984. *Rebellion in tne Veins: Political Struggle in Bolivia, 1952-1982.* London: Verso.

Echuazú Alvarada, Jorge. 1983. *Los problemas agrario campesinos de Bolivia.* La Paz: Published by author.

Engels, Frederick. 1968. "Letter to F. Mehring, July 14, 1893." In *Karl Marx and Frederick Engels: Selected Works.* New York: International Publishers.

Fondo Internacional de Desarrollo Agricola (FIDA). *Mission especial de programación a la República de Bolivia: Propeustas para una estrategia de desarrollo rural de base campesina.* Report no. 0006-BO. 2 vols. Rome: FIDA.

Foster-Carter, Aiden. 1978. "The Modes of Production Controversy," *New Left Review* no. 107 (January-February):47-78.

Friedman, Jonathan. 1974. "Marxism, Structuralism, and Vulgar Materialism," *Man* (London) 9 (September):444-69.

Giddens, Anthony, and David Held, eds. 1982. *Classes, Power, and Conflict: Classical and Contemporary Debates.* Berkeley: Univ. California Press.

Goodman, David, and Michael Redclift. 1981. *From Peasant to Proletarian. Capitalist Development and Agrarian Transitions.* Oxford: Basil Blackwell.

Harding, Timothy F. 1982. "Critique of Vanden's 'Marxism and the Peasantry. . . , ' " *Latin American Perspectives* 9 (Fall):99-106.

Harris, Richard L. 1978. "Marxism and the Agrarian Question in Latin America," *Latin American Perspectives* 5 (Fall):2-26.

Hindess, Barry, and Paul Hirst. 1975. *Pre-Capitalist Modes of Production.* London: Routledge and Kegan Paul.

Hurtado, Javier. 1986. *El katarismo.* La Paz: Instituto de Historia Social Boliviana (HISBOL).

Ibarra Grasso, Dick Edgar, and Roy Querejazu Lewis. 1986. *30.000 años de prehistoria en Bolivia.* La Paz: Los Amigos Del Libro.

Instituto Latinoamericano de Investigaciones Sociales (ILDIS). 1985. *Debate agrario.* vols. 1-2, *Hacia una segunda reforma agraria.* La Paz: ILDIS.

_____. 1986. *Debate agrario,* vol. 3. El agropoder. La Paz: ILDIS.

Katz, Friederich. 1972. *The Ancient American Civilizations.* Trans. K. M. Lois Simpson. New York: Praeger.

Kearney, Michael. 1984. *World View.* Novato, California: Chandler and Sharp.

Kelley, Jonathan, and Herbert S. Klein. 1981. *Revolution and the Rebirth of Inequality: A Theory Applied to the National Revolution in Bolivia.* Berkeley: Univ. California Press.

Kendall, Ann. 1978. *Everyday Life of the Incas.* (paperback) London: B. T. Batsford.

Klein, Herbert. 1969. *Parties and Political Change in Bolivia: 1880-1952.* London: Syndics of Cambridge Univ. Press.

_____. 1980. "The Structure of the Hacendado Class in Late Eighteenth-Century Alto Peru: The Intendencia de La Paz." *Hispanic America Historical Review* 60 (May): 191-212.

Ladman, Jerry R., ed. 1982. *Modern-Day Bolivia: Legacy of the Revolution and Prospects for the Future.* Tempe: Center for Latin American Studies, Arizona State Univ.

Larson, Brooke. 1980. "Rural Rhythms of Class Conflict in Eighteenth-Century Cochabamba," *Hispanic America Historical Review* 60 (August):387-406.

———. 1983. "Shifting Views of Colonialism and Resistance," *Radical History Review* 27:3–20.

———. 1988. *Colonialism and Agrarian Transformation in Bolivia: Cochabamba, 1550–1900.* Princeton, NJ: Princeton Univ. Press.

Larson, Brooke, and Robert Wasserstrom. 1983. "Coerced Consumption in Colonial Bolivia and Guatemala," *Radical History Review* 27:49–78.

Liss, Sheldon B. 1984. *Marxist Thought in Latin America.* Berkeley: Univ. California Press.

Lora, Guillermo. 1975. *La masacre del Valle Cochabamba: Enero, 1974,* 2nd ed. La Paz: Cuadernos Justicia y Paz.

———1977. *A History of the Bolivian Labour Movement; 1848–1971.* Edited and abridged by Laurence Whitehead. Trans. Christine Whitehead. Cambridge: Cambridge Univ. Press.

Lukács, Georg. 1971. *History and Class Consciousness.* Trans. Rodney Livingstone. London: Merlin Press.

MACA and Food and Agriculture Organization of the United Nations (FAO). 1982. *Informe: Consulta de expertos sobre indicadores socio-economicos para el seguimiente y la evaluación de la reforma agraria y el desarrollo rural en America Latina.* La Paz: MACA and FAO.

Malloy, James, 1970. *Bolivia: The Uncompleted Revolution.* Pittsburgh: Univ. Pittsburgh Press.

Malloy, James, and Eduardo Gamarra. 1988. *Revolution and Reaction: Bolivia, 1964–1985.* New Brunswick, NJ: Transactions Books.

Malloy, James, and Richard S. Thorn. 1971. *Beyond the Revolution: Bolivia Since 1952.* Pittsburgh: Univ. Pittsburgh Press.

Mariátegui, José Carlos. 1971. *Seven Interpretive Essays on Peruvian Reality.* Austin: Univ. Texas Press.

Marx, Karl. 1964. *Pre-Capitalist Economic Formations.* Ed. Eric J. Hobsbawm. New York: International Publishers.

———. 1977. "Results of the Immediate Process of Production." In *Capital: A Critique of Political Economy.* Vol. 1. ed. Ernest Mandel. Trans. by David Fernbach. New York: Vintage Books.

Meillassoux, Claude. 1981. *Maidens, Meal and Money: Capitalism and the Domestic Community:* Cambridge: Cambridge Univ. Press.

Ministerio de Asuntos Campesinos y Agropecuarios (MACA). 1971. *Curso nacional sobre comercialización agricola en el proceso de reforma agraria.* La Paz: MACA.

———. 1978. *Centro regional de investigación para la reforma agraria.* La Paz: Consejo Nacional de Reforma Agraria (CNRA) and MACA.

Mitchell, Christopher. 1977. *The Legacy of Populism in Bolivia: From the MNR to Military Rule.* Praeger Special Studies in International Politics and Government. New York: Praeger.

Mojica de Camacho, Emma. 1978. *Resumen del estudio de la estructura agraria en Bolivia.* La Paz: Consejo Nacional de Reformat Agraria (CNRA) and Ministerio de Asuntos Campesinas y Agropecuarios (MACA).

Murra, John. 1986. "The Expansion of the Inca State: Armies, War, and Rebellions." In *Anthropological History of Andean Polities,* ed. John Murra, Nathan Watchel, and Jacques Revel.

_____. 1980. *The Economic Organization of the Inca State.* Research in Economic Anthropology, Supplement 1. Greenwich, CT: JAI Press.
Nash, June. 1979. *We Eat the Mines and the Mines Eat Us: Dependency and Exploitation in Bolivian Tin Mines.* New York: Colombia Univ. Press.
Pearse, Andrew. 1972. "Peasants and Revolution: The Case of Bolivia," Parts I and II, *Economy and Society* 1 (August and November).
Platt, Tristan. 1986. "Religión andina y conciencia proletaria" *Fe y Pueblo* 3 (August): 31–35.
_____. 1987. "The Andean Experience of Bolivian Liberalism, 1825-1900: Roots of Rebellion in 19th-Century Chayanta (Potosi)." In *Resistance, Rebellion, and Consciousness in the Andean Peasant World; 18th to 20 Centuries,* ed. Steve J. Stern. Madison: Univ. Wisconsin Press.
Poulantzas, Nicos. 1973. *Political Power and Social Classes.* Trans. Timothy O'Hagen. London: New Left Books.
_____. 1978. *Classes in Contemporary Capitalism* Trans. David Fernbach. London: Verso.
Reinaga, Fausto. 1971. *Tesis India.* La Paz: no publisher.
Resnick, Stephen A., and Richard D. Wolff. 1987. *Knowledge and Class: A Marxian Critique of Political Economy.* Chicago: Univ. Chicago Press.
Riester, Jurgen. 1975. *Indians of Eastern Bolivia: Aspects of their Present Situation.* Internation Work Group for Indigenous Affairs (IWGIA) no. 18. Copenhagen: IWGIA.
Riordan, James, Stephanie Wilson, and Corey Yulinsky. 1983. *Análisis de la encuesta nacional socioeconomica del sector agropecuario boliviano, 1978.* Estudio de politicas agropecuarias, no. 2. Spanish trans. Fernando Garcia E. and Haydée Delgardo U. La Paz: Ministerio de Asuntos Campesinos y Agropecuarios de Bolivia (MACA) and United States Agency for International Development (USAID).
Rivadeneira Prada, Raúl. 1984. *El laberinto politico de Bolivia.* La Paz: Editorial Cinco.
Rivera Cusicanqui, Silvia. 1978. "El mallku y la sociedad colonial en el siglo XVIII: el caso de Jesús de Machaca, *Avances* 1 (febrero).
_____. 1979. "La expansión del latifundio en el altiplano boliviano," *Allpanchis: Revista del Instituto de Pastoral Andina* (Cuzco, Peru) 12 (No. 13):189–218.
_____. 1983. "Luchas campesinas contemporáneas en Bolivia: El movimiento 'katarista,' 1970-1980." In *Bolivia, Hoy,* ed. René Zavaleta Mercado. Mexico City: Siglo XXI.
_____. 1984. *Oprimidos pero no vencidos; luchas del campesinado y qhechwa, 1900-1980.* La Paz: Instituto de Historia Social (HISBOL) and Confereración Sindical nica de Trabajadores de Bolivia (CSUTCB).
_____. 1985. "Apuntes para una historia de las luchas campesinas en Bolivia (1900-1978)" in *Historia Politica de los campesinos latinoamericanos,* Vol. 3, ed. González Casanova. Mexico City: Siglo XXI.
Rodríguez O., Gustavo. 1980. "Original Accumulation, Capitalism, and Pre-capitalistic Agriculture in Bolivia," *Latin American Perspectives* 7 (Fall):50–66.
Rojas, Antonio. 1980. "Land and Labor in the Articulation of the Peasant Economy with the Hacienda." *Latin American Perspectives* 7 (Fall):67–82.
Romero Pittari, Salvador. 1982. "The Role of the State in the Rural-Urban Configura-

tion." In *Modern Day Bolivia,* ed. Jerry Ladman. Tempe, AZ: Center for Latin American Studies.

Semo, Enrique. 1987. "Ideology, Scientific Thought and History," Trans. Susan Casal Sánchez. Photocopy.

Spalding, Karen. 1975. "Hacienda-village relations in Andean society to 1830," *Latin American Perspectives* 2 (Spring):107–21.

Stern, Steve J. 1982. *Peru's Indian Peoples and the Challenge of Spanish Conquest: Huamanga to 1640.* Madison: Univ. Wisconsin Press.

———. 1983. "The Struggle for Solidarity: Class, Culture, and Community in Highland Indian America," *Radical History Review* 27:21–45.

———. 1985. "New Direction in Andean Economic History; A Critical Dialogue with Carlos Sempat Assadourian," *Latin American Perspectives* 12 (Winter):133–48.

———. 1987. *Resistance, Rebellion, and Consciousness in the Andean Peasant World: 18th to 20th Centuries.* Madison: Univ. Wisconsin Press.

Taussig, Michael. 1980. *The Devil and Commodity Fetishism in South America.* Chapel Hill: Univ. North Carolina Press.

Thompson, E. P. 1966. *The Making of the English Working Class.* New York: Vintage Books.

Urioste Fernández de Córdova, Miguel. 1984. *El estado anticampesino.* Cochabamba: Instituto Latinoamericano de Investigaciones Sociales (ILDIS) and Cinco.

Urquidi, Arturo. 1970. *Las comunidades indigenas en Bolivia.* Cochabamba: Los Amigos del Libro.

Vanden, Harry E. 1982. "Marxism and the Peasantry in Latin America: Marginalization or Mobilization?" *Latin American Perspectives* 9 (Fall):74–98.

———. 1986. *National Marxism in Latin America: José Carlos Mariátegui's Thought and Politics* Boulder: Lynne Rienner Publishers.

Vilar, Roberto. 1981. *El trabajado agricola y la migración temporal en Santa Cruz.* La Paz: Oficinia Internacional de Trabajo (OIT) and Fondo de Naciones Unidas para Actividades de Población (FNUP).

Vilar, Roberto, and Carlos Samaniego. 1981. *Sistema de contratación laboral temporal en Santa Cruz, Bolivia.* La Paz: Oficina Internacional de Trabajo (OIT) and Fondo de Naciones Unidas para Actividades de Población (FNUP).

Wachtel, Nathan. 1977. *The Vision of the Vanquished: The Spanish Conquest of Peru through Indian Eyes, 1530-1570.* New York: Barnes and Noble.

Whiteford, Scott. 1981. *Workers from the North: Plantations, Bolivian Labor, and the City in Northwest Argentina.* Austin: Univ. Texas Press.

Wolf, Eric R. 1969. *Peasant Wars of the Twentieth Century.* New York: Harper and Row.

———. 1982. *Europe and the People Without History.* Berkeley: Univ. California Press.

Wolpe, Harold, ed. 1980. *The Articulation of Modes of Production: Essays from Economy and Society.* London: Routledge and Kegan Paul.

Wright, Eric Olin. 1978. *Class, Crisis and the State.* London: New Left Books.

Zagha, Roberto (Misson Leader). 1984. *A World Bank Country Study: Bolivia: Agricultural Pricing and Investment Policies.* Washington, DC: World Bank.

Index

Acción Democrática Nacionalista (ADN), 76
Achuqualla, 110
Agrarian Reform, 3, 28, 70, 71, 85, 88, 106, 113, 120, 121, 131
Aguirre Gainsborg, Jośe, 64
Alejo Calatayud, 132
Alianza-MNR, 76
Anaya, Ricardo, 65
Arce, José Antonio, 65
Ayllu, 34, 36–40, 44, 49–51, 86, 106, 110, 130
Aymaras, 1, 2, 14, 48, 73, 78, 89, 95, 96, 103, 104, 110, 111, 113, 130
Ayni, 111

Banco Agrícola Boliviano (BAB), 79
Banco Central, 64, 77
Banco Minero, 64
Banzer, 75–77, 79, 81, 91, 93, 115
Barrientos, René, 74–76, 120
Bartolina Sisa, 132
Bolivian state, 59–61, 66, 69–73, 103, 119–122, 131–134
Bravo, Fernando, 63
Busch, Alberto Natusch, 80
Busch, Germán, 63

Campesino
 definition, 3
 relation to indígena, 4
Cardenas, Víctor Hugo, 121

Cataví massacre, 65
Centros Operativos del Agropoder (COAs), 122, 133, 134
Chaco War, 60, 61, 106
Class
 definition, 9, 15–17
 E. P. Thompson's definition, 107
 intermediary class, 9, 22, 31–33, 40, 42, 45, 101, 116, 120, 122, 129, 132, 133
Coca, 1, 113
Collective memory, 102
 long horizon, 103
 short horizon, 103
Communal relationships, 110
Comuneros, 110
Comunidades, 48, 50, 96, 109, 113, 114, 122
Confederacíon Nacional Trabajadores de Bolivia (CNTCB), 74, 76
Confederacíon Obrero Boliviano (COB), 71, 75, 78, 79, 81, 82
Confederacíon Sindical de Trabajadores Bolivianos (CSTB), 65
Confederacíon Sindical Unica Trabajadores Campesinado de Bolivia (CSUTCB), 73, 76, 78, 79, 101, 104–109, 115–117, 119, 121, 122, 127, 132, 133
 political thesis, 79, 104–106, 119
Corregidor, 49

Exvinculación, 50

141

Faena, 110
Falange Socialista Boliviana (FSB), 64
Fausto Reinaga, 74
Federacíon Sindical de Trabajadores Mineros de Bolivia (FSTMB), 63, 66, 79, 81, 82
Flores, Genaro, 73, 74, 76, 79

Garcia Meza, Luis, 79
Gueiler Tejada, Lidia, 79
Guevara Arze, Walter, 65
Gulf oil, 74

Hacendado, 47, 50, 51, 59, 62, 70, 86, 87, 106, 112
Hacienda, 31, 33, 47, 48, 50–53, 61, 62, 69–71, 85–87, 89, 109, 110, 122, 131, 134
Hertzog, Enrique, 67

Ideological state apparatus, 20, 22, 23, 26
Ideology, 12, 14–20, 22, 24, 26, 31, 32, 37–41, 43, 45, 46, 48, 53, 60, 61, 71, 83, 86, 96–98, 101, 102, 108–110, 115–118, 120, 127, 129–131, 133, 134
Immediate process of production, 10, 15–22, 25–27, 32, 102, 109, 117, 127–129, 133
Inca, 9, 10, 25, 26, 34–42, 45, 50, 66, 78, 83, 86, 97
Indígenismo, 73, 98, 105, 108
 postrevolution resurgence, 73
International Monetary Fund, 77

Jilaqata, 50
Julián Apasa, 46, 130

Katarista, 14, 27, 45, 76, 83, 102, 103, 105, 107, 108, 115, 116, 118, 121, 132
Kuraka, 9, 22, 28, 33, 36–38, 40, 42–46, 48, 49, 52, 53, 86, 132

Lara, Jesús, 117

Lechín Oquendo, Juan, 113, 121, 149
Lora, Guillermo, 63, 64

Mariátegui, José Carlos, 105
Massacre of Tolata and Espizana, 75
Migration, 33, 72, 85, 89–91, 93, 94, 110, 111, 114, 115, 118, 122
Miners, 3, 47, 53, 59, 60, 63–69, 71, 74, 78, 80–82, 114, 118
 thesis of Pulacayo, 63
Mining
 big three, 64
 decline, 81
Mit'a, 26, 37, 38, 50, 110, 207
Mode of production
 definition, 2
 articulation of modes, 2, 4, 9, 11–14, 21, 23, 26, 28, 31–34, 50, 52, 53, 83
 loose articulation, 53
 tight articulation, 52
 subsumption, 22, 52, 53, 85–88, 97, 118, 131, 243
 formal, 52
 real, 52
Movimiento indio Tupaj Katari, 74
Movimiento Nacionalista Revolucionario (MNR), 3, 60, 61, 63–72, 75, 76, 85, 102, 103, 105, 112
Movimiento Revolucionario Tupaj Katari, 74
Movimiento Revolucionario Tupaj Katari-Liberación (MRTK-L), 121
Movimiento 15 de Noviembre, 73

National Revolution, 59, 64, 65, 67–69, 85, 102, 103, 105, 114, 115, 122
Navarro, Gustavo Aldolfo, 64, 105
New Economic Policy, 82

Ovando, Alfredo, 74

Pachamama, 97, 112
Pacto Militar, 74, 78, 129
Partido Comunista Leninista, 77
Partido de Unificación Republicana Socialista (PURS), 67
Partido indio de Bolivia, 74

Index *143*

Partido Socialista Obrero Boliviano (PSOB), 105
Partido Socialista Uno, 74
Paz Estenssoro, Victor, 60, 65–68, 70, 72, 74, 77, 81–83, 120, 121
Peasantry
  National Indigenous Congress of 1944, 62
Peñaloza, Luis, 65
Pionneer communities, 109, 111, 112
PIR, 64, 65, 67
POR, 63–65, 67, 68, 80, 105
President Mariano Melgarejo, 49
Primo de Rivera, José, 64
Proyecto de Ley Agraria Fundamental, 121

Quechua, 1, 2, 48, 78, 89, 91, 95, 96, 102, 103, 110, 112
Quevedo, Ramos, 62
Quintanilla, Carlos, 64
Quiroga Santa Cruz, Marcelo, 74, 79

Raymundo Tambo, 73
Razón de Patria (RADEPA), 65, 70, 105
Recaudadores, 49

Reinaga, Fausto, 73, 106
Repartimientos de mercancías, 42, 43, 46, 47
Rosca, 60, 61–65, 68, 70

Salamanca, Daniel, 61
Sexino, 67
Siles Suazo, 68, 69, 72, 76, 79–81

Tejada Sorzano, José, 64
Tomás Katari, 46, 132
Torres, Juan José, 74
Túpac Amaru, 45, 46, 64
Túpac Amaru II, 46
Túpac Katari, 46, 73

Umaraqa, 110
Unidad Democrática Popular, 76

Villarroel, Gualberto, 62, 63, 66, 67

Willka, Pablo Zárate, 50, 52, 53

Yanaconas, 51